CP isn't me

Samantha Maxwell

ISBN 9798356681622

Wordworx Wrexham Enterprise Hub
11-13 Rhosddu Road Wrexham
LL11 1AT

CP isn't me

Samantha Maxwell

S. Maxwell

"A dedication in loving memory of my wonderful Nan, Mary Jane"

Foreword

How do you define Cerebral Palsy? Moreover, how do you define disability in general?

I can imagine that CP is more difficult to describe, let alone define, as you may not be aware of the different forms of disability; indeed, many understand the term 'disability' as one 'universal' thing. I can imagine that this may be easier for you to try to describe? Disability as a single word can be generalised as being something that needs extra care and help. You may see a wheelchair and identify a person in that wheelchair as needing attention in or needing help on a regular basis to live for example. The truth is, disability has many different forms and levels, alongside different levels of care requirements that crucially need to be highlighted in order to enhance and improve knowledge of this subject. Not all disabilities are the same.

My intention is to highlight this concept. It may seem 'too heavy' to deal with just from the first paragraph, but I am not prepared any longer to be blanketed by disability, and neither should any

Foreword

other person living with a disability of some description. It is a part of life, but so are the different levels and forms of disability. The sooner people realise this and change their attitude and approach to this, the better.

It strikes me that abilities are not questioned for able-bodied individuals, yet abilities are always questioned when disability is thrown into the mix. Everyone has different levels of ability, regardless of if they possess a disability or not. Everyone is good at something. Able-bodied persons abilities are referred to as 'skills' or a specialist 'skill-set' and it is acceptable. When a disabled person's abilities are questioned, then we are deemed as needing extra help. Whichever way you decide to look at it, you cannot deny this is a form of discrimination. I can imagine that you have never thought about ability in this context before?

This is why a book of this nature desperately needs to be out in the world. To highlight the facts and try to clarify some misconceptions of disability that need to be realised.

Ready? Let us begin

Chapter 1
Introduction

A book like this should never have to be written. Everything in this book comes down to common sense. The general public hasn't got this message it seems, though. So I'm going to take it upon myself to see if I can change people's minds about what it means to be disabled. But I shouldn't have to.

If you do your research, Cerebral Palsy or 'CP' is said to be 'a group of disorders which affect a person's mobility through their balance and posture'. Cerebral Palsy is the most common disability in childhood which refers to a person's motor skills. 'Cerebral' refers to the brain. 'Palsy' refers to weakness or issues using the muscles. I agree with this definition to a point as this is a somewhat accurate definition of CP. It provides the facts of what is known about the disability. It doesn't, however, reveal the truth of what life with such a disability actually looks like in reality.

A disability is said to be something which interferes with a person's ability to do general everyday activities. However, this definition (in most cases)

Introduction

isn't entirely correct as it infers that disability puts a stop to any chance of a normal, independent life. It doesn't necessarily, but this definition consequently has a knock on effect with the public as they then believe that all disabled people are weak. It's like this for all definitions of all disabilities. I know this from conducting research to write this book. Not to say there aren't more severely disabled people out there. Of course there are, and they may need a little more help and that's fine. It's trying to separate fact from fiction, and I feel fiction is winning over fact. This ends now. I have fought hard to achieve what I have achieved regardless of how books or the Internet say I should be. I've broken down those barriers to some extent on a personal level, having a proper mainstream education, going onto higher education and taking it upon myself to find proper employment – which is extremely challenging if you have a disability of some form - take it from me, I know. People shouldn't be so quick to judge a person just because they may have a disability. It's horrible. People may think they are being understanding, but they are being understanding for completely the wrong reason. We need it to be understood that whatever is said in books or on the Internet, we need to be seen as capable and independent people. We need people to give us some sort of chance of life, like every other person. I really do believe that a person's physical appearance shouldn't be the main focus. The main focus should be on a person's abilities, full stop. When I was growing up, because of the disability label, I was automatically seen as weak, so much so that I wasn't allowed to try to do things for myself (in school especially.) For a long time – and I talk more later about this, I was put into special needs classes and even a special needs school at one point just because of what was known about disability. I wasn't allowed to be independent. I had to have support workers in class. Everywhere I went, a support worker had to follow, which was fine, I adapted later into the mainstream classes, but I always had to have a support worker at the side of me just in case something happened. I used to look at other pupils in class and around the school and wonder why they didn't have to have a support worker, but I did? It was a label that I didn't want, need or deserve.

I think that such a label automatically puts a person at a disadvantage, as others may think that person needs constant help, and as a result, a perfectly capable disabled person has their independence taken away in a shot. Let's look at this in more detail

Introduction

for a second. It's important to be independent whether you are disabled or able- bodied. Every single individual living in the world deserves independence. It teaches forward- thinking and learning about life. How the world works, and how you work. If you are independent, you can make your own choices. What you like, what you don't like, and being able to identify themselves and become able to do so without others interfering. You wouldn't deny the opportunity for independence to a toddler, learning to walk, talk, read, write - all of these things, for example, are seen as a right of passage to lead an independent life. Why should a person who just so happens to have a disability be treated any different? I would assume giving a disabled person the opportunity to live a more independent life is only a good thing. It makes the person feel useful and in charge of their lives, their confidence will grow massively and they will will have a much greater knowledge of how to take care of themselves to a point. By always doing things for a special needs person, I am sorry to say this but you are in fact making the situation worse. A disabled person who does not have the chance to explore and experience their own independence will become dependent on others and unknowledgeable of how the world works. They will become reliant on 'more capable' people, which is not the best for anyone, whether able-bodied or disabled. The able-bodied person will not be able to have a break or a life themselves as the constant wants and needs of the special needs person will take over - through no fault of their own, I may add. It has been drilled into the disabled that they didn't need to be independent as others will always be there to do everything for them. Nobody lives forever. What would a disabled person do if their primary care giver passed away or injured themselves? Without having the wonderful chance to discover independence, a special needs person's life will be nothing more than an existence reliant upon others. That's no way to live in my personal opinion. Therefore, it is so important to promote independence, and even more so for special needs individuals. How would you like to be seen as inferior everyday and as a result, unnecessarily losing your sense of independence and therefore your identity? You just become a shadow of yourself with absolutely no exploration of your personal abilities whatsoever. You are treated like a robot in many cases. You have lost who you really are, or what you potentially could become; all because of some small minded individuals who, in part, I personally feel, simply cannot grasp the

Introduction

ideas of disability and independence. The subjects don't go hand in hand. How does that feel? It doesn't feel that great I imagine? Of course, you're only imagining it; for a disabled person, it is a million times worse, as they are living it everyday of their lives. Trust me, I have lived it, and still am living it in many ways depending upon the people I come into contact with.

Expecting a disabled person just to go along with whatever your limited mind thinks it means to be disabled is discrimination, whatever way you look at it. I'm the same as you in terms of knowledge and capability. Yes, I may need help in some areas of my life (as everyone does from time to time I may add) but that doesn't give someone the right or the power to condemn me to a life of feeling unworthy of a normal life. Every single disability is different. It's time now to put everything you think you know about disability into a pile and burn it, and try to rethink disability for what it actually means in reality compared to how it is written as fact, because it is not fact. We are not a statistic, we are people with our own personalities. The sooner people realise this, the better. After all, that is why there's a Disability Discrimination Act nowadays, to make sure we are treated fairly, as equals and more than that, as human beings.

The definition of discrimination in terms of disability is when a person who is living with some form of disability (it doesn't matter what form) is treated unequally, unfavourably, or not even given the same opportunities as other able-bodied individuals, all because of their disability.

I have been treated with discrimination from an early age. Having to attend a special needs school specifically for disabled children when I was young, and having to put up with some negativity. I have been patronised and bullied just for how I look, both in school (secondary school) and in past workplaces. Those setbacks can have a negative effect on a 'normal' person's mental health, never mind a disabled person's mental health. All of which I describe in more detail later, but the fact remains that discrimination of disability exists, whether you choose to believe it or not, it is part of everyday life. The sad fact is that most people are unaware of their discriminatory attitudes and actions towards the disabled. Again, most think they are helping by not letting us explore our independence, or act in such a way that in fact

Introduction

belittles us. Exclusion is a major factor when discrimination of disability is happening. For example, and again, I go into more detail on this later, I was denied the opportunity to participate in sports days in secondary school because of my disability. I had to sit on the side-lines in my wheelchair watching everyone else having fun and enjoying themselves.

To be denied opportunities that other able-bodied people have is awful. People shouldn't be stigmatising us over something we can't control, it's like we're being punished, we deserve to be offered the same opportunities as other, more able-bodied people. You should look past our disability and see the real us. Our personalities paint a different story to what we are seen as being or by what a book says we are. The amount of misery and anxiety that a person with a disability can feel over how they may be seen is both overwhelming and unnecessary.

I believe that research into the different forms of disability isn't always correctly made, and this is why there is virtually no change in attitudes. A great deal of research that is out there is one- sided. Research never covers all bases of disability. The good, along with the facts (or what is written as fact). Only half the truth is known. The whole truth needs to be discovered and discussed properly as there are still gaps in how people should behave when with a special needs person. Nobody knows how to handle such a situation and when able-bodied people are in a position to interact with a disabled person, their automatic reaction is to either patronise the special needs person, or worse, ignore them completely. It is far easier to do this. Out of sight, out of mind right? It's easier for people to accept an invisible condition than accepting a physical condition. Maybe because invisible conditions aren't up in people's faces everyday so they can turn a blind eye to these conditions, but they cannot move past the physical? It doesn't make sense to me. General society wraps disability into one block and automatically discriminates. I am absolutely sick and tired of being labelled, of people not taking me seriously just because I'm a wheelchair user, I don't know what people think will happen if they have to interact with me. I don't know, because I'm not them. I am me. Wheelchair or not, nobody should be discriminatory towards anyone. We are all the same. I don't understand how one little difference can impact a person's thoughts so much.

Introduction

The blame isn't squarely pointed in the direction of society, as they are only doing what they are told or have been taught by what information is out there. The information needs to change, then maybe people's attitudes may change if and when they read the truth of disabilities and realise how 'normal' we actually are. If the time was put into actually researching the many different forms of disability thoroughly, looking more deeply into each condition separately and doing deeper research into each disability's potential abilities once and for all instead of just looking at the negatives of what each disability may bring, then I believe that we will be half way there to accepting disability for what it actually is. It's nothing to fear, nothing to be judged by. Disability is just another way of living. It's something to be celebrated in a positive way. Let us now have the conversation without shying away from it. To include everyone, we need to be shutting the door on the stigma of disability.

There is finally a starting point however...

The way disability is portrayed through the media is beginning to become more visible. Although it has been a long time coming. Society is now able to finally see disabled people on TV, whether actors, presenters, comedians, also sports personalities. Social media also uses disabled models on clothing brands, or disabled entertainers, which is an extremely important and incredible thing. The door has finally opened up (and about time too!) However this isn't enough. I personally feel that disability is still seen in a negative light in general society. Far more should be done to turn the tables to give disability a chance. That one thing is education in schools.

The amount of backlash I've faced just because I sit in a wheelchair is a lot to say the least. There's something in the mindset of the public that make it the belief that disabled people can only be disabled and that's it. It's our role and responsibility to 'act' and 'be' disabled; we are not allowed to be anything more (that goes against what disability is, after all). The question however is, what if we don't want it? What if we're tired of the same thing of people talking slowly as they think we have no understanding of a situation or what is being said to us? What if we're just sick of playing the victim? What if we just want to be us?

Even my personal experience of the healthcare sector has been disgusting from time to time with

Introduction

regards to not being allowed anything (on occasion) as it would cost money. My family had to fight for everything in order to enhance any possible chance of self independence. It's not right that they had to fight for everything, on my behalf (even a pair of specialised scissors that I used in school,was seen as asking too much!). When I was young, I couldn't grip a pair of normal scissors to cut with, so I used a specialised pair of scissors. Instead of the scissors having looped handles, these handles were flat, which meant it made it much easier to cut with as I would put pressure on the bottom of said scissors using my hand, instead of using my fingers to try and cut with. My school at the time, suggested to mum to get a pair through the healthcare sector as it was thought the scissors would be beneficial to assist with my development. Needless to say that the sector refused to give me a pair of these scissors due to budget cuts. As soon as the school found out, they gave me a pair of scissors, as they couldn't believe I was denied such a small thing due to budget cuts.

I had a disability bike when I was young, it helped to exercise my muscles in my legs and I felt normal. Of course the bike was not provided by the health care sector due to budget cuts, so mum and dad bought a second hand disability bike for me. I loved it! As time went on, I inevitability grew, just like other 'normal' children grow, who knew? So the bike wasn't safe for me to ride any longer. For years after, I went without the bike that gave me freedom and independence. It was not until I was in my teenage years when I was offered a bike by the hospital. I couldn't believe it! I was actually getting my freedom back after so long! I went to the hospital to try the bike out, making sure it fitted properly. After trying the bikes, we went away, but never heard anything more from the hospital about the bike and I'm still waiting to this day.

As I grew older, the house needed adaptations to suit my changing needs. Fights with local authorities would happen due to not having a disabled parking bay for my mobility car. I think this is why I am so fed up now of local authorities, etc., as I was denied so much of which I needed in order to enhance my life. Eventually, this was resolved by a local councillor after months, even years, of unnecessary stress and anxiety on my family. We now have a disabled parking bay along with other needed adaptations to the house, including a downstairs wet room and through-floor lift in order for me to access to my bedroom.

Introduction

I am not going to sugar-coat it either. There are hidden costs to being disabled as the equipment is unnecessarily expensive. Why should it cost so much just for a person with special needs to live an independent life? I do feel that these companies take advantage of people in my situation and charge as much as they can get away with as they know we cannot live without said equipment. The attitudes of people who claim to have a higher level of power is awful sometimes, they think they have a hold on you because you rely on them to help you get the things you need to live a relatively normal life. It's just horrible the way you can be treated, there aren't any words to describe this level of arrogance.

I need to write about something now which ties in nicely to what I've just said. I feel it needs to be discussed to hopefully show you how hopeless this was in reality. I'm talking about the assessments special needs people had to take part in to prove that the disabled were in fact actually disabled. It was just ridiculous the way both the assessments were handled, alongside how people's lives were handled.

For a complete stranger to come into your home and judge you on your abilities, is just cruel. In some cases, these people were cruelly misinterpreting the situation. The level of questioning was basic. There was no attempt made to scratch under the surface and look at all aspects of disability.

People with special needs do have different levels of ability. Some can do more than others. Not all disabilities can be considered or categorised the same. It's awful to think so. Some people are able to walk, talk and do other things that could be considered 'normal' by a superficial society. Not all disabilities are visible either, not every disability confines a person to a wheelchair. The sooner this is realised and put into practice in terms of treating every person equally, the better.

To be incorrectly denied the basics decreases a person's level of independence and their self esteem and is utterly unacceptable.

Authorities, (in my personal opinion) just look for loop holes in order to deny people their rights to have an independent lifestyle. By assessment standards for example, if you were able to do most everyday activities without too much difficulty, you were at risk of losing your benefits. The assessment simply trivialised and generalised disability into this

Introduction

one group, the questions were never set to include the different forms of disability, therefore the assessments never told the full truth of all disabilities separately. If the assessments considered every disability separately, then the results would have been very different, I personally feel, by giving the people who required disability benefits their entitlement, and saying no to the chancers – which is what these assessments were designed to do in the first place. Instead, it ended up being a battle in many cases for disabled people to keep what was rightfully theirs to begin with. All that I am saying is if authorities had taken the time to look at the bigger picture of a special needs person's lifestyle, looking at ALL areas of their life on a daily basis, and most importantly, listening to them, it would become clear that benefits are needed in order to enhance any possible chance of self independence, self-growth and esteem. These strangers were not there to see what it's like for us on a daily basis in regards to self care for example. These strangers just made a judgement on our lives based on basic questioning which had nothing to do with helping the disabled. We felt as if we were in a zoo, having to perform for the public. It wasn't right to be treated like that.

As a result, many special needs people had their benefits snatched away, including equipment and mobility vehicles, purely because we were able to do most things such as lift our arms above our heads for example. In many ways, we felt as if we had to hide our true abilities and become more severely disabled just to please these people and claim our rights to live as independently as possible.

I did anyway.

We had to be careful in what we said and how we said it, in case we said something wrong, otherwise our benefits would be ripped away in a second.
I personally had to face one of these assessments. It wasn't the best experience to say the least. Some stranger came to the house and I was subjected to an hour of unrelated questioning towards both me as an individual and me in terms of my disability. I felt like I was being tested, and if I failed one of the questions, my life was virtually over, I had no other means of income. That is how unnecessarily invasive the assessments were.

On paper, the assessments seemed to have a good reason why it needed to be done. The assessments

Introduction

were put in place by Government to determine who needed disability benefits and who did not. It's no secret that some able-bodied people access disability benefits without needing them as an attempt to live an easier life without the need to work. People who think it's okay to take advantage of things that are there to help the people who definitely need these things to live are just awful individuals. Why would anyone do that, or feel comfortable to do things such as that? It's beyond me. That's when disability is acceptable, when people can cheat the system to claim what isn't rightfully theirs. These benefits are not there for anyone to use. These benefits are there in order to help a special needs person's quality of life, to enhance their independence. It's not a free- for-all. We definitely do not have it easy. We come against discrimination and judgement every single day. We want to be able to work, but there are two types of reasons why a disabled person isn't working and needs benefits. One, these people simply cannot work because of their form of disability. Some disabilities are more severe than others and they are unable to work. Two, the public makes the decision for us. We are seen as being unable to work just because we have a condition. It's easier for society to say that our disabilities makes it difficult for us to work as I think the word alone scares the majority of people. This is something that I have experienced in the past and I elaborate on later. It is an horrible experience though. Unless you are on the receiving end of such an awful experience, I don't think anyone truly can understand the embarrassment and sense of worthlessness that comes with this.

I cannot help but think that if able-bodied people didn't apply for benefits, special needs people wouldn't have been made to go through it at all. The people who were sent out to people's homes had no idea of disability. There was absolutely no compassion, no form of understanding, just discrimination. Our dignity was taken from us, having to undergo such a thing.

When my own assessment was made, I just felt as if I was being punished for my disability, as if my condition wasn't severe enough to even be considered a disability. It was disgusting how I was treated as I felt like I was in the wrong for being disabled. I, or any other disabled person should never have been made to feel uncomfortable or guilty for having a condition of some form.

Introduction

Some special needs people as a result had their benefits taken away from them as they were deemed by law to be 'able to work' to get a regular income. Special needs people may have underlying conditions that may not allow them to work. Government grouped people together without any knowledge of what being disabled means. It wasn't their responsibility. If you were seen to be independent in most activities, you were able to work, in the eyes of Government anyway. There was no doubt in their minds.

Again, Government should have made it their priority to look at every situation separately and properly in a well thought out manner, taking into consideration a person's feelings of having to prove to a stranger to be disabled, when so clearly it's obvious that we in fact are, then maybe the backlash may not have happened. I understand the Government may have been trying to cut corners as there's a lot of disabled people living in the UK, and as a result they may have been trying to save money, but the reality is the Government may have ultimately lost money trying to put right what went so wrong in the first place. I don't really know, I'm just surmising, but I do think something like this happened during this time as it was so obviously wrong the way the assessments were carried out, there's no other logical reason or explanation in my opinion. As special needs individuals were made to feel inadequate by such an experience, of course that level of backlash was always going to happen.

The idea was great. The execution of the idea needed to be rethought. Those assessments were never correctly thought out to include someone's feelings. The assessments were there to make people feel ashamed of who they are. Putting into question their sense of value and belief in themselves. Your level of ability should never be the target for judgement. Ability should be encouraged, never be made to feel in any way shameful. This is how I felt at the time. I felt like I had to hide my level of ability in order to keep the benefits I was entitled to.

Disability isn't something to feel ashamed of. Disability is a normal part of life. We should never be made to feel inadequate, especially by someone who doesn't know us and what it actually means to be disabled It's time people realise this as fact.

I don't actually know if the assessments still need to be done, if they do, then these assessments do

Introduction

need to be reconsidered to include every single individual disability and not generalise it as one thing. I cannot stress this enough.

The assessments need to be reassessed.

I felt I needed to write about this now, in the beginning of the book, as it is an important issue that needs to be addressed and taken seriously, sooner rather than later.

These are just three examples of many - I will expand on other personal battles that both my family and myself have had to face just to give me a slice of an independent life later on in the book - but what I will say for now is the struggles have been unnecessary. It's almost as if the healthcare sector never wanted me to thrive. They wanted me to be a stereotypical disabled person, it seemed. It was easier for them to say no, and put the money they saved towards more 'important' things. What could be more important than giving a disabled child a chance not to be excluded from everyday activities? I can say now after so many years of being treated as invisible, that I have rights, I'm a person just like everyone else, I deserve to be treated with respect and dignity. I deserve inclusion. I deserve acceptance. I deserve independence. I deserve to live. You cannot put a price on that. It's disgusting behaviour if a higher authority decides that you are not as important as their latest community build project. It's a form of discrimination. I know the powers that be may not like that discrimination label, but neither do I like to be labelled as disabled, and the same goes for every other disabled person living on the planet. I'm proud to be disabled, like so many others the same as me, I just don't like what negative ideas can come with it. It's horrible to have to deal with it. We have enough to contend with in our everyday lives with discrimination, we don't expect to have to deal with it from the places that are supposed to be there to help us. I did have a hatred of the healthcare sector at one point as they only got in touch, it seemed, to explain what they couldn't do; it was never what they could do. Their whole attitude was negative, there was never a positive word. I just really want to make it clear within this book that disability never means you have to surrender to your condition. It never means your life has to be limited. It's the people around us who doubt our abilities who make our lives limited. I was made to feel unimportant and because of this, I felt like I never had a voice. What I thought never

Introduction

mattered to the healthcare sector. The way it made me feel - I wouldn't wish it on my worst enemy.

More recently, the healthcare sector has taken notice and has been more involved. Going from literally no help whatsoever to all of a sudden having to be on call in case there's a sudden appointment is a turn up for the books. It's quite unbelievable and if I am honest, a bit overwhelming. I had forgotten what it meant to have people constantly at your door. I'm not complaining about it, it's just a bit of a shock to go from no help to suddenly be bombarded.

When a special needs person reaches the age of eighteen, you are seen as an adult, so all of that support is gone completely in an instant. I'm not sure why this is, but it is a fact.

Mum recently had to apply for me to have support again from the healthcare sector, and this is why I am finally getting what I deserve, but it should never have to come to that. Child services should continue into adult services. It is logical. Support should remain for people living with conditions, regardless of age. I had it explained to me that if I don't constantly ask for help from the healthcare sector I am seen as 'unproblematic' and as a result I fell off the radar. There are two departments, child and adult. These two departments never speak to one another which is a problem as a child grows into an adult, regardless of ability, but this does not seem to be taken as fact by the healthcare sector, as many people who have a condition seem to be disregarded unless they make a fuss. It is extremely important that care should never be taken away from a person just because they are a certain age. You cannot turn off disability in most cases. We need that care in order to enhance our independence and thrive. We are not second class citizens. We deserve and are entitled to a life full of opportunities. If you remove our rights to live independently as an adult, then you are nothing more than evil. We deserve to be happy and live our lives to the fullest. Care must carry on throughout our lives without it being cut off when a person living with a disability reaches the age of eighteen.

However, I spoke about the importance of independence and also the fact of always helping is taking away our independence. When I speak about care, that is a whole different story. Care from the healthcare sector is there to help a person be

Introduction

as independent as possible. Always giving help unnecessarily prevents independence. I just wanted to make it clear of the difference between care from the healthcare sector to enhance independence with equipment to make our lives easier for example, and constant help from everyday people that can put an end to a disabled person's independence. You are going read a lot about the difficulties and challenges that come with being seen and treated as disabled. Alongside other challenges due to mental health, talking about my own personal experiences and battles with my mental health, and also talking about the recent pandemic and subsequent lockdowns, I have decided to write the book like this as I believe that it maybe more relatable to special needs people to read and to show them that there can be some light at the end of the tunnel if they have experienced anything I am going to speak about in the book, and prove to everyone else that disability does not make a person weak. If anything, it makes them stronger.

This book is mainly going to focus on Cerebral Palsy, which is the condition I personally have. This however doesn't mean, nor will it ever mean I'm not 'normal'. I'm going to write about my life, the good and bad times to give you some idea on disability, and prove to everyone how normal we truly are, also giving you something to think about in terms of how everyone wrongly treats disability and try to change your minds on how to improve your ways to make disabled people feel included, which is all we really want, need and deserve.

Disability is obviously going to be the subject of the book. Let's however start with Cerebral Palsy.

Cerebral Palsy can take three main different forms (to my knowledge) mild, moderate and severe. I personally have the mild form of the condition which basically means, I have mobility issues, but I can do various everyday activities and can also be quite independent - when allowed.

Like I said before, I do get very annoyed when I am patronised by people who think I don't have coherent thoughts. Not to offend any other person with a mental disability, I'm well aware of the struggles and frustrations people face on a daily basis who live with a condition such as this. In particular, as I've known pupils in school who deal with something like this, and how annoying it is for

Introduction

said individual to have people realise that they just want normality too.

Miscommunication and misunderstanding is the most heart-breaking, yet it is a common thing for most people who are living with a disability. Why is this? Again, I personally think it comes down to lack of knowledge about the word 'disability.' Just that word alone. We shouldn't focus on the negatives of said word (the prefix - dis) but focus on the latter part of the word (-ability.) Every person is good and capable of something, disability or not. That is fact. I do believe in making disability a part of the school curriculum as it is a normal part of life. We desperately need it to be a part of the educational system to stop any fear or misconceptions that the topic can have in the thoughts of the public, replacing it with understanding, acceptance and inclusion, we need to focus on the positives that a person with a condition can bring to the world, instead of always focusing on the negatives. It gets tedious after a while, trying to prove your worth.

For me, since I was young, I knew that I wanted to do something creative with my life, so I fought tooth and nail to achieve those dreams and I became a graphic designer, a job which I love for two reasons. One, I am actually creating things that customers want and need, which are designed by someone who is disabled, and two, the sad but more appreciative reason of acceptance - finally being accepted for who I am in a genuinely equal working relationship. That is the most important thing for me as it wasn't easy to get to where I am today. Not by a long shot.

You see, the cause of Cerebral Palsy is due to a lack of oxygen to the brain whilst the baby is developing in the womb. Knowing this now, I can imagine you feel sympathetic? Not to be ungrateful for any form of support you may think that you are giving by being sympathetic, but please don't be. Please don't waste your sympathy on me, or any other person living with a disability. I personally don't need or have any desire for any sympathy that is given to me. I have the mild form of Cerebral Palsy but that doesn't mean that I'm any less worthy of a normal life. I've gained all of the qualifications, including the graphic design degree I needed, and I have finally found the job opportunity that I have been searching for, one that at long last doesn't discriminate in any way, shape or form. I am not restricted by my CP. So this should not give you the right to patronise me, I also don't want or need that

Introduction

undignified "bless them" attitude as I'm a person just like you; please do not treat me any differently from anyone else. It is extremely important to realise that disability, no matter the form of a condition, should not change the way a person is seen in society. We are the same as everyone else. We just need to be able to prove it.

Questions can be asked when an able-bodied person sees a disabled person acting 'normally'. After all, it doesn't seem right does it? I can imagine that when you think of the word 'disability' or 'disabled ' your mind automatically thinks of a wheelchair or something such as this, with the view that we are unable to do things, am I right? It is okay if your brain went to the general view, after all, it is how you have been programmed to believe. Things associated with disability are our trademark. This is why we desperately need to turn disability into something more positive, not just a barrier, blocking inclusion, making us feel uncomfortable, but it shouldn't become something to shy away from either. Every disability is different, moreover, everyone is different, but our differences make us the same. We need to realise that disability just means we live a little differently than any able-bodied person. We can have the capability to achieve most things others do, we are fed up with the same misconceptions, we need to be realised as an individual who has a disability, rather than being constantly labelled and referred to as 'disabled' and that be it. We are much more than just disabled.

The common questions and statements people with special needs are constantly asked are, "What can I do to help?" Or, "It's okay, I'll do that for you." Maybe the best thing someone can do is to understand that a person with a disability is the same person as them. I sound like a broken record, saying the same thing over and over again but it is important not to treat them differently simply because they have a form of disability. Never believe disability means weakness. We are far from weak. You cannot move passed our physical appearance. You are unable to view us as normal because let's face it we're not . We look different and that scares people. For many, the only way to overcome this sense of being scared is being patronising, which in my opinion has become a part of modern culture almost. Almost everyone is patronising towards the disabled. It's how society is taught. It's their default, sadly. Patronising behaviour is never good. It just causes anxiety and hatred for the person who is only trying their best

Introduction

to 'help.' This 'help' however is only caused by what is written down. However, this 'truth' needs to be removed from social consciousness for the actual truth to be written and put in replacement of what is being believed currently.

It's fact that disability is treated as a life limiting thing when it definitely isn't. The number of times I've come across people who feel sorry for me because I'm physically disabled, how it's a 'shame' that I'm disabled, is annoying. Unless people are willing to take the time to re-educate themselves on this subject (and this goes for mental health too, which will also be discussed later), then there is no hope for people. There just isn't. I believe that if people are willing to be re- taught, then discrimination will be stopped once and for all. I've had to let people know that despite my disability, I went to college and university, got my qualifications and I'm now a graphic designer. The shock on these people's faces when they are told this is unbelievable. Disability and making a life for yourself is something that people cannot connect. It's not right from what they understand disability to be. Disability is what you make it. If you have the capability, why not push yourself to achieve more? This backwards thinking needs to end. It's up to the

40

person though whether they want to be re-educated, I will never force anyone. I couldn't. It's their choice, but it's also our choice to be asked to be treated normal. Everyone is entitled to the right of a normal life , whatever that means for an individual. Why can a person with a disability gain such popularity in media, but people are so quick to judge a person in the street just by how they look. Why? The only explanation that I can think of is that people on TV and social media are on TV and social media. What I mean is it maybe easier to distance yourself from any contact that you may have to experience when coming into contact with a disabled person. You don't have to make conversation (God forbid), with said person. There is a barrier when watching TV or on social media. A screen. A screen gives people 'permission' almost to either enjoy what is being shown or unfortunately bullying behaviour to start, disability or not. Actually seeing a disabled person in the street can be uncomfortable to most people and I do wonder why this is. We are normal (whatever normal is). We have feelings, we bleed, fall in love, cry, laugh, everything that regular people convey and do, believe it or not, disabled people share the same life as everyone else in the world. For many, this is a difficult thing to accept. Talk to a person

Introduction

with a condition as you would anyone else. Let us be as independent as possible by letting us try to do things ourselves before you offer help, if we don't try, we will never learn. We would be much more appreciative if we were treated like normal human beings instead of feeling like we're second class citizens everyday of our lives. Get to know us before you label us unnecessarily, and above all, just treat us with respect and equality without talking down to us. That is literally all we want, need and deserve. Just because we may look different from you, sound different from you, or do things a little different from you, it doesn't mean our minds are the same as our disabilities. Just because something is true on paper, it doesn't mean it's true to life. Look at the person in question. Never judge us on our initial appearance. In other words, never judge a book by its cover, treat people how you want to be treated. I'm repeating myself, but I think it's needed to repeat myself to get this important point across.

Of course there is that one thing that disabled people may have to face. That one thing can be a something to affect a disabled person which affects their minds and confidence, and that one thing is bullying. Bullying behaviour is not acceptable.

Whether it's physical, mental or through social media. How do I know? Well, I have been bullied, not physically, but mentally whilst in high school. This bullying has stayed with me to this day, I believe that my mental health became worse during these years. I will go into more detail later. What I will say for now is that bullying behaviour in any context is not right, whichever way you look at it. Research I feel is to blame for this discrimination and bullying. All there is in books and on the Internet is the different forms of disability and how negative disability is; we cannot do a lot if you take it as fact. We're useless. These are the misconceptions that take place when reading up on disability in general. It's not actually society's fault. If it's written down, it's surely the gospel right? Wrong. Nothing written should be assumed to be the truth. This is just information that can be a factor, but everyone is different, every disability is different. Disability affects people in different ways. The research into disability is a guide, it doesn't mean that every person with a condition needs to have every single symptom of their particular disability. It's strange to think so. For example, I have a mild form of Cerebral Palsy as said before, I can talk and do most everyday activities without too much difficulty as mentioned above. Other

Introduction

people with Cerebral Palsy can walk, but others may have trouble with speech, and others simply cannot do anything at all. Now do you see what I mean? Every person is different. Every disability is different. Every capability is different. I just want to hammer that point home. Bullying causes a person to question why they are targeted, develop mental health issues that can carry on into later life (as it did with me), and unfortunately in some cases, depending on the level of the bullying, causes a person to question if it's all worth it. (I don't think I need to spell out what I'm saying here.) Adding disability into the mix is just cruel. We can't help how we are. We have enough to deal with without anyone making it worse. We didn't ask to be disabled but it is what it is, we cannot help how we are, but we are still human, we are still living, no matter how people view disability, we are not, in any way, prepared to take what is being either said, done or written about us anymore. We do need more education into disability in school I think. Black history is finally being taught in schools, which is a major, positive step forward to educate people to be more accepting, which is fantastic; so why can't disability be added to the mainstream school curriculum? By doing so, disability can be also taught in a positive way. The different levels of disability, teaching how each condition is written down, but also teaching how normal disability really is in reality. Having children look into disability and normalising it will hopefully make people more understanding to put an end to discrimination and bullying for good. My Cerebral Palsy does not make me any less worthy than the next person. I can literally do almost anything that anyone else can do, but just because of my wheelchair, I feel as if I'm restricted to a life of being labelled as disabled. I hate it, I'm not going to lie. This is why I think that education will help to achieve a greater understanding of disability alongside the different levels of ability of a disabled person.

Most issues I've faced in life so far are misunderstanding and miscommunication, patronising behaviour and just a general sense of worthlessness which, just like I said, disabled people face on a daily basis. It's sad but true that this is the case. Attitudes definitely need to change, we are living in the twenty-first century after all.

I'm going to go into more detail later in this book talking about my own personal experiences and the struggles that I've had to go through in my own life, both on a personal level and a disability level

Introduction

(trying to get people to understand that I'm much more than my CP, and the struggles I've had trying to get that fact across to people, this is what I mean about my struggles, not struggles in terms of my actual disability, as I have learned to adapt my life to be independent, but trying to get people to change their minds about me). It'll be an extremely therapeutic and cathartic experience for myself to actually get it written down physically after having carried these thoughts and feelings around for years.

My main mission is to give some understanding to those who may need it without actually knowing that they need it. To learn about yourself, and how your behaviour affects a special needs person. Hopefully after reading, you may be more able to recognise how your words and actions towards disabled people can hurt. The patronisation ends today. The avoiding ends today. The bullying ends today. The exclusion ends today. Every single thing that makes a disabled person feel useless and worthless ends today. I'm not sorry for what is in this book. It needs to be said in order for change to finally happen. There's been enough tiptoeing around the subject, I want to hit it head-on for this discrimination to stop. You may not think of yourself as being discriminatory, people never do. Try to think how awful it is for a person who happens to have a condition of some form being treated like a second class citizen. It's not a great feeling is it? This is why I need to write this, to stop the negativity on a daily basis that we face. We deserve better. Enjoy the book, but learn something from it, and adapt your attitudes in a positive way. After all, we need to start somewhere.

Writing this, and pouring my heart out, talking about things that I haven't before, will become worthwhile if this helps just one individual with a disability, helping them to realise that their disability isn't them, it doesn't define them, they define who they are with their personality and ability. If it also helps at least one able-bodied person become aware of their behaviour, becoming much more educated on the subjects that matter to change their views, not letting what is written or initial sight of a disabled person cloud their opinion. If just one able-bodied person becomes more aware and willing to change their attitude, if that happens and makes at least a small positive change, then it will be a job well done in my own opinion. It will not be an easy read by any stretch of the imagination, but a book like this needs to be out there to hopefully show you how normal we actually are.

What you are about to read and have already read above are all my own thoughts and feelings around CP and disability. I'm not going to say that these thoughts and feelings are shared with other disabled people, I'm just trying to get across my story, what negativity I've faced and what I've witnessed others have faced who are in the same position as me. I cannot speak for every disabled person on the planet, I'm not a mind reader, I'm just trying to make it clear that discrimination of disability does happen as I have been subjected to it and have seen others being subjected to it. It desperately and definitely needs to stop. I hope you enjoy this book and it opens your eyes to the full picture of disability and goes some way to end the discrimination for good. Be open-minded when reading, grow and learn about your actions towards the disabled community. We are not just our disabilities, we are so much more.

Chapter 2
Facts and Myths

Before we begin, please know that all of the following are a mixture of experiences on a personal level alongside more in-depth research taken from reputable sources from books and medical websites. I am disabled, but I'm no expert, even on my own personal condition of CP. I have learned a lot from doing research into my own condition. I cannot take any responsibility or credit for what I am about to write in chapter two, for the most part.

Generalised View

Firstly, before anything else, let's actually look at what is written as fact about CP alongside disability in general in order to help educate everyone a little more on the subject, and if necessary, bust some negative ideas of Cerebral Palsy and disability in general along the way.

As I mentioned earlier, I personally have the mild form of Cerebral Palsy which basically means that I have mobility issues, but I also am able to participate in most everyday activities with little to no difficulty.

Facts & Myths

This book mainly concentrates on my own personal journey with the condition, therefore I am mainly going to concentrate on this form as this is the form I know inside out, and feel more comfortable sharing my own personal opinions.

Let us firstly look at these facts and myths of disability generally.

There are approximately fourteen point one million people who have some form of a disability (according to my research). This is unbelievable given how common the subject should be, yet isn't. The amount of discrimination which we face on a daily basis is way too much considering the fact above. You would think that because there are so many of us living with a disability, there would be more of an accepting attitude. Sadly, for the majority of us, there isn't.

Many disabilities are invisible such as MS, ADHD and autism, as well as others. You don't need to appear physically disabled to be given that title, so many disabilities do not require a wheelchair, or only require a wheelchair sometimes for certain parts of their life, taking long journeys, for example.

Disabled access toilets are not just for wheelchair users. This is another common misconception. If a person's disability makes it difficult to stand for long periods and need a hand rail to help them to stand, and/or they have a colostomy bag, which means they may need extra space, privacy, and running water to help, then accessible toilets are there to assist these types of situations too. It's to give a sense of dignity to a person who has a form of disability. It's not okay for able-bodied people to take advantage of these accessible toilets when they were designed for people with conditions. I've had this happen to me, having to wait for the toilet designed for my needs to become vacant because an able-bodied person thought it was alright to use it themselves. It's just unacceptable and I can't find a logical reason why anyone would do this if they do not need to use a disabled toilet in the first place. I'm asking every able-bodied person to think before you act and not to use a disabled toilet as it is more 'convenient' for you. You are taking away our independence if you do.

There is another thing that takes away our independence. Vehicles parked by dropped curbs or on pavements, obstructing our access. We like to be seen as normal, but how can we be when a vehicle is parked next to a dropped curb or parked on the pavement? It may seem trivial, but dropped curbs are there for a reason. That reason is to give people with disabilities a sense of freedom. Having a vehicle block our path is blocking our right to live a normal life. Pushchairs and buggies also have the same problem. Please be aware of this when you park your vehicle. Don't deny us our independence.

Many people who live with a disability have had to deal with some sort of prejudice. We are seen to be less able than other 'average' people. So much so that disabled people are twice as likely to be unemployed compared to able-bodied people. We are 'too stupid' for want of a better term, to work. Our minds can't handle the pressure that a job can bring. That's just wrong. This is something that I have unfortunately experienced, whilst trying to find employment in the past, which I will talk about more later. The ironic fact is people living with some form of disability are extremely unlikely to take time off from work. It seems to me that employers are unwilling to hire special needs people because they think that these people will take a lot of time off due to their disabilities. This is ridiculous. Disabled employees stay with their place of employment much longer than the 'average' person. We are so grateful for an employment opportunity we are never going to let it slip from our fingers.

Putting to one side the cost of housing, the number of working age people who have some form of disability and are living in poverty is much higher than the number of working age able- bodied individuals.
It is said that disabled people living in some form of poverty is twenty-six percent, whereas able- bodied people living in some form of poverty is twenty-one percent. I found this information from the Scope website. It's disgusting that we should be allowed to live in some form of poverty just because of who we are. It's the discrimination that we face that causes this poverty in my opinion. If able-bodied people weren't so quick to judge us, I can imagine that poverty figures would lower significantly.

If employers would be more accepting of disability, then the benefits of that opportunity for a disabled person will ultimately positively impact both the employee and employer. This may also lead to lower percentages of poverty as the disabled would have the funds to secure a more stable future for themselves.

Facts & Myths

Never be scared of the word 'disability'. We are more able than society gives us credit for. Be the person to go against the grain and hire a person with a condition, no matter what the condition is. If a disabled person is capable to work and wants to work, give us an opportunity to prove it. That's all we ask. I shouldn't have to say this, it is common sense to let everyone have the same opportunities as others, a person's appearance shouldn't matter, if someone has the capability, capacity and ability to do things in more or less the same way as others, why should there be discrimination?

My point is, our disabilities should never get in the way of ourselves. Our personalities make us who we are. Our abilities make us who we are. You should look at us. The world would be much better if we were more tolerable of everyone.

I am now going to speak about the specific facts and myths of Cerebral Palsy. Just to explain, there are other facts and myths of different conditions, but as I personally have CP, I feel more able to discuss this condition as this is the condition that I know more about. Take these facts and myths of CP and try to rethink what you may already know about disability in general, because although CP has different symptoms to other forms of disability, think of the facts and myths of Cerebral Palsy as learning about disability in general as this maybe a starting point of disability becoming more accepted in everyday society. However, never make the mistake of thinking that the facts and myths of Cerebral Palsy cover disability as a whole. Different conditions have different facts and myths attached to each of them. Use the facts and myths of Cerebral Palsy that I'm about to speak about as a guide to do your own research.

Cerebral Palsy Facts and Myths

It is widely believed that Cerebral Palsy is a condition a person is born with. In actual fact, CP can happen at any time in life to anyone. Contracting an infection (meningitis for example), having a stroke, or a severe head injury can all be causes of the condition.

Delays in major milestones as an infant can be considered the most common sign of the condition. Milestones such as sitting up unaided by eight months old, difficulty in crawling, and lack of

Facts & Myths

walking by the age of eighteen months are some key examples to take note of.
This is what I experienced in my early years and it made my family aware of something that wasn't quite right as my mum explained this exact time to me many years later, when I asked.

I was diagnosed with the mild form soon after by the Paediatric consultant at the hospital.

Other signs of Cerebral Palsy are, the body being either extremely stiff or extremely floppy, depending upon the individual. Weak legs and arms (my left arm is significantly weaker than my right arm. The control pad on my powered wheelchair is on the left hand side to supposedly strengthen the arm to be just as strong as the right arm). More signs of CP are muscle spasms (which I have myself), fidgety and jerky movements, tremors in the hands and for individuals who can walk whilst having CP, doing so on their tiptoes.

In more severe cases of the condition, there may be difficulty in swallowing and feeding. Drooling is another sign of the condition. Having constipation, difficulty in speech and general communication skills, (I could be considered as having this as sometimes it's difficult for me to express myself). Developing epilepsy, interrupted sleeping patterns or complete lack of sleep, scoliosis, (again I have this; it's actually a curvature of the spine). Hip joints that easily dislocate, learning disabilities, (half of the people who have Cerebral Palsy have a learning disability of some form.) Bladder control issues, issues with vision including limited vision, rapid eye movements or in some cases, developing a squint. Loss of hearing is yet another sign of Cerebral Palsy. All of these 'signs' or 'difficulties' however, should never be misinterpreted as a sign of inner weakness.

My own personal experience has lead to a greater sense of inner strength, ready to prove to anyone who questions or challenges my abilities, wrong. My own personal condition consists of lack of physical mobility, however, I am able to stand and take a few steps if someone is with me just in case I fall on my face! Sometimes I have difficulty in expressing myself verbally, so I find it easier to either email or text someone when having to contact an individual, rather than using a phone but I can speak to someone face to face. It is the phone I have difficulty with as I get flustered on the phone. When I have to talk on the phone, I have to give mum permission to speak on my behalf. I've tried speaking on the phone before, let's just say I just can't do it. I use a straw for drinking as I'm uncomfortable trying to pick a cup up. As I said before, my control pad on my powered wheelchair is on the left hand side to try and encourage my left hand to become stronger in order to match the strength of my right hand. I need help with personal care, but that's all. Everything else I can do myself.

My parents were told, when I used to go to the hospital to see how I was developing with my Cerebral Palsy, that I would never gain weight because basically, even though my legs do not work in a normal way, all of that energy that people put into walking, my legs will automatically put that energy into my metabolism. If I eat something, my legs will quickly burn off the excess calories in order to keep me at a constant weight. It's known as 'palsy skinny.' To put it another way, due to the extra energy we use, people with different forms of Cerebral Palsy with high muscle tone and regular spasticity, like I have, have naturally 'slim' bodies throughout their lives. This is dependent on said individual, however, and not always the case.

I remember talks were made during my last year of secondary school for me to have a course of Baclofen which is basically a muscle relaxer. The thought was to try and lower the amount of spasms that I have in a standard day. It was either going to be injected through my spine or taken orally. After research, it was decided that I would not have the treatment as the side effects outweighed the benefits. I would have to watch what I ate as it would reduce the amount of spasms, so basically I would gain weight that would have been difficult to lose, I'd become drowsy, and with my GCSE's coming up, it wouldn't be the best idea.

Another form of treatment was discussed soon after, that my physiotherapist could do. This was Bowen technique. Basically it's a massage of the muscles, re-aligning them in order to minimise any pain I sometimes have. This was better as I just had three treatments every so often during physiotherapy which never interrupted my studies at the time. I'd feel as if I was able to concentrate better as the pain in my joints were gone for a while. I still have this form of treatment to this day from time to time when I feel it is needed, of course I have to pay for it myself now, but it's worth it as the amount of relief after treatment is wonderful.

Facts & Myths

I've spoken about the facts of the condition, using what is known about CP in general and using my own experience of living with Cerebral Palsy on an emotional and personal level. Now let's talk about the myths of the condition, the things that are thought of as fact when Cerebral Palsy is brought to the forefront of conversation, when these facts aren't true to the person. I'm going to number each myth in order to hopefully show them clearly and to make my point clear that the myths are exactly that, myths, and should not in any way, shape or form be accepted as fact.

CP mainly affects movement and posture, and as previously discussed, only half of people with it have a learning disability. This level of learning disability can vary from mild to severe. This however is dependent on the severity of the condition for an individual. Most people with CP can expect to enjoy a life filled with different opportunities to expand their education without worry.

One in four people living with CP are unable to speak. This minority of people find other ways to communicate, however, through methods of technology, using voice assisting equipment for example. The rest of us are able to speak and are able to hold a conversation.

The majority of people with Cerebral Palsy are healthy and can expect to live for as long as the average person in the general society. People who have the condition are also able to live independently and enjoy long careers if so desired.

Most children who have Cerebral Palsy are healthy and enjoy a meaningful education, and participate in both hobbies and sport. Their quality of life should not be hindered in anyway just because they have CP.
There is absolutely no evidence to suggest that CP affects fertility. Since the condition is not hereditary, a woman who has Cerebral Palsy can be expected to carry a baby to full term and have the baby the same way able-bodied women have children.

I have only listed these facts and especially the myths as a way to show you and highlight what is already known and to try and get you to see the condition in a new light. Cerebral Palsy can take many forms, but not all of the above can be attached to every individual who has the condition. It could be as subtle as it was with me in my early years in terms of not reaching the milestones of walking or sitting up without help. It doesn't mean we aren't strong-willed, it just depends on said individual and what their abilities turn out to be. I think that the biggest disability in life is the misconception that disabled people are just on this planet to be disabled and nothing more. It seems a criminal offence in a way if we want to educate ourselves to get a job and lead a relatively normal life. This is what I personally discovered as time went on. Being judged constantly over something I have no control over is the most belittling thing I have experienced.

You can easily put this down to discrimination in many regards. I'm not an expert so I've had to do some research on the Disability Equality Act of 2010. I'll briefly describe the act in layman's terms.

Essentially, the act establishes that as a disabled person, you have rights in order to give disabled people a level of protection against discrimination. The rights that are covered by the act relate to areas including employment, education and dealing with the police. I do wish that I had known this both in my early years and later in life to give me some backup to metaphorically stand up against all of the people who have showed a form of discrimination towards me. It would have saved me a lot of mental health issues in doing so.

I love 'normal' everyday experiences such as shopping, cinema trips, family days out, spending time out with friends, attending concerts and festivals - just standard everyday activities, because guess what, I'll let you into a little secret, I am actually normal. It's just society likes to label me with something of greater severity than I actually have.

I have Cerebral Palsy, Cerebral Palsy doesn't have me.

Mental Health Facts and Myths

I have just gone through the facts and myths of Cerebral Palsy, which hopefully will help you to understand the condition a little more.

As my own mental health has suffered throughout the years due to the discrimination of my CP, I'm now going to go into the facts and myths of mental health. In order to enhance the subject matter of this book, it is only fair and important to highlight

Facts & Myths

the facts and myths of mental health. Drawing from my own experiences. It is a misconception that only certain people suffer from a mental health issue of some kind. This of course isn't true. Anyone can suffer from a form of mental health. Depending on your lifestyle, mental health doesn't discriminate and can fluctuate during the course of a person's lifetime. We all can become stressed or anxious about situations we find ourselves in. Sometimes that level of stress or anxiety can lead to further distress and can cause deeper mental health issues in some cases. Nobody is exempt from mental health issues.

Practising good mental health can help to minimise the risk of issues, of which I will go into more detail later in the book.

Just because you are unable to visualise a mental illness, it's never any less, in shape or form, painful or debilitating than a broken limb for example. Issues with mental health can feel just as bad, or even worse (depending upon a person's mental state at the time), compared to a physical illness. A mental health issue sometimes isn't treated with the same level of understanding or support as it's not visible to the naked eye. It is unacceptable to not take mental health seriously. The problem is, it is not in the mainstream. Saying that, if mental health was more exposed, I really cannot imagine that the subject would be properly researched either. It would just become another elephant in the room just as the subject of disability is, acknowledged, but with no clear understanding. Nobody likes to think they aren't understanding when it comes down to the 'heavy' topics, but from personal experience, I can tell you that people say they understand, but they don't, not really. Everyone acts sympathetic, but their level of sympathy does not prove their understanding. This does need more exposure in order to enhance support for individuals who need help when they ask. With the right support, people can recover to a point from a mental health issue. It's just finding that support that people need. Mental health (like disability) can be considered a taboo subject. People never want to admit that they may need help for fear of ridicule or misunderstanding, which of course isn't the right message.

Mental health issues are common. So much so, you may know someone who is living with a mental health issue, but you may not even realise it as they are hiding it to give the illusion of happiness. The

Facts & Myths

fact is that one in five people experience some form of a mental health issue during their lifetime. Most people with a mental health issue of some form are in work and can hold down a job. Again, as with disability, it is misunderstood that people who are living with a mental health issue cannot work. The fact of the matter is, you may well be working with someone that has a mental health issue.

Suffering a physical injury does not make a person weak; nor does living with some form of a mental health issue. Again, a mental health issue is a common part of life and can happen to anyone, from any background. Many high-profile, successful and inspirational people have experienced a mental health issue and many gain strength from the experience. Look at it this way, an injury does not make a person weak; with the right support, people can recover from their injury and become stronger. Conversely, the pressure to become successful; either by personal pressure to achieve, or the outside world piling on pressure to succeed, may lead a person to develop a mental health issue. Never be ashamed to ask for help. By asking for help, you may gain some inner strength to overcome your mental health issue, you may even inspire others to do the same.

I suffer from my mental health and I've learned the only way to try and take back some control is by talking about it and getting help. It's definitely not easy to do, I hid my mental health problems away from as many people as I could for a long time, until one day it all came to a head. I'm lucky in the sense of having people around me who understand and also having a release in writing this book. Unless you take back control, your mental health will control you. I talk more later about this but I just want to make this clear to you as I feel it's important.

The facts and myths of Cerebral Palsy and mental health is just a small part of what desperately needs to be done and taken seriously. I've started the ball rolling. There are many more facts and myths into different forms of disability and mental health. I've only scratched the surface. It's up to you to research more into the different levels of both subjects.

Until both subjects are taken seriously, alongside the subject of disability in general, we run the risk of just becoming a society of discrimination. It's up to you to do further research. Disabled people can

Facts & Myths

only do so much to try to change the minds of society. At the end of the day, why should we?

Why should we have to change your minds about how you view us? It's not our job. It shouldn't even be the case that I have to write about something as normal as disability and mental health. However, we are where we are unfortunately. It's society's job to be accepting of disability and mental health.
It is up to you.

Chapter 3
Younger Years

When I was a child, I didn't really know that a disability could be thought of as something negative. I didn't really connect my disability to any negatively whatsoever. Why would I? I had a normal life, living with my family who were made up by at the time by my mum and dad, my older brother and sister Ian and Leanne, my dear nan and my lovely little Yorkshire Terrier, Bubbles (I'm a major Michael Jackson fan!).

I actually remember when mum and dad said that we were getting a dog, I was so excited! I instantly fell in love when I first saw Bubbles! I decided I wanted him. There was an instant bond. Bubbles just became part of the family. He never went into kennels, as I wasn't prepared to leave him on his own when we were on holiday. We would have to book pet friendly accommodation so we could take him with us. If Bubbles couldn't be with us for some reason, nan would look after him until we returned home, and uncle Alfie would go to nan's house twice a day to walk him. She would always keep in contact with me to put my mind at rest and tell me

Younger Years

what he did that day and how he was as he was my baby, as I worried when he wasn't able to come on holiday. I used to call Bubbles my little pumpkin as he was born around Halloween. Every Halloween I used to dress him in his little pumpkin costume, complete with hat, and he'd just wander around the house all evening dressed as a pumpkin! Whenever I felt ill in the night as a child, with the usual childhood illnesses, Bubbles would instantly jump off the bed (as he used to sleep at the bottom of my bed by my feet) and tap the bedroom door until mum came in to look after me. Bubbles was amazing. The bond we had was incredible.

This was the little family unit I had for a good few years and I loved every second of every day. I had other family members including my auntie Christine alongside my cousins and my granddad Irving on my dad's side. My nan's siblings, great auntie Lizzie and great uncle Stevie were also a part of my life at the time. We used to visit great auntie Lizzie from time to time with nan and great uncle Stevie used to give me a pound coin whenever he saw us in town. This part of my family I saw as my extended family.

My granddad Alf (nan's husband and dad to my mum and uncle,) and my nanna (granddad Irving's wife and mum to my dad and his sister, my auntie Julie,) both sadly passed away when I was one year old, (within six weeks of each other actually, from what I understand,) so I didn't really know them that well sadly.

This however didn't deter from the amount of love and support I felt in abundance from my immediate family. My family made me normal. There was absolutely no question in my mind that I was different in any sense. We spent every hour of every day together, especially my brother and myself.

We were virtually inseparable in our childhood, there's actually nine years age difference between us, Ian was (and still is, in many ways, with his own children) a big kid at heart and I think he loved it when I came along as he had someone to act stupid with. I always looked up to him as he just accepted my disability from the get go, not letting any part of my disability become an issue. We used to watch films together, 'Ghostbusters', 'Toy Story', 'The Simpsons' 'Wallace and Gromit' and 'Star Wars' were favourites in particular, and are still my favourites to this day, and we would just generally

Younger Years

be together as much as possible. His sense of humour is what I remember the most from those first years of life. We used to laugh and just be as stupid as much as possible together and I loved it! I just always wanted to make Ian proud from an early age.

From a very early age, I went to the Wrexham Maelor Children's Centre twice a week, with other special needs children (all of whom had different forms of disability), where my development was monitored through the guidance of the physiotherapist. It was after several months that my diagnosis of mild Cerebral Palsy was confirmed by the paediatrician, which was first suspected in my GP appointment as the reason why I wasn't developing normally, (or hitting the milestones) of a regular child.

When I was two and also at four years old, I had to go to Cardiff for a fortnight for physiotherapy to a place called Bobath. (The Children's Centre arranged it and the local authority at the time agreed to fund the two week placement on both separate occasions). With the added pressure of budget cuts today, I consider myself extremely lucky and grateful to have been given the opportunity twice, only two years apart. By attending Bobath, I learned hand - eye coordination alongside other abilities to make me as independent as possible. The centre was opened to look at different methods to enhance a child's quality of life and also their self esteem. Basically it was a more intense look on how they could improve a child's abilities to give them a better lifestyle in the future with as much independence as possible. Each session was catered to the one child. It wasn't as if we were grouped together, every child was different with different abilities and capabilities in their eyes, so each session was adapted to each child individually. Mum, dad, Ian and myself went down to Cardiff during my first placement. For the second placement, it turned into a bit of a family holiday as nan and Leanne came also alongside Ian, mum, dad and myself.

I had videos from those days and Ian was there in the physiotherapy sessions helping in any way he could to get me to do the tasks that were set for me. He was, and still is, an incredibly amazing older brother and important part of my life as he helped me to develop and normalise me in some ways. I'll never forget what he unknowingly did in giving me the confidence to be who I am now.

I didn't really spend that much time with my sister Leanne from what I can remember growing up as she moved out when I was young, with thirteen years difference in age it was a bit more of a struggle to find things in common but she was always there in my life in some way. I do remember, however, that we used to have 'baking Sundays', where we just baked cakes all day and I used to eat the left over batter from the mixing bowl! She used to paint my nails from time to time, play with my ears to get me to sleep at night (which still works to this day) and give me makeovers using her make-up. I attended the hospital with other disabled children where we would learn motor skills for life. I remember Leanne took me swimming once with the hospital. She took me in the water as she was a confident swimmer, it made me confident also.

I loved both her and Ian greatly growing up and I still do. They will always be my older brother and sister no matter what.

Mum and dad have given me everything they could in order to give me a relatively 'normal' life. I never wanted for anything growing up. Everything I wanted or needed, my parents made sure I had. They were and still are extremely loving and supportive. They do their very best to make me happy, even to this day. They are still there when I need them. I do just want to say to them that I do appreciate everything you did when I was young and everything else you continue to do now to try and make me happy. I love you both so much.

My dear nan was just fun! That's the only way to describe her. She taught me how to make a cup of tea using a metal tea set which I now have. We would sing using her extremely old tape recorder, we would make pancakes in her kitchen, but the very best thing was (Ian can vouch for this, as it's his favourite now) after school, going to see nan and she would give me a slice of coconut cake. It's the simple memories that can hold the greatest amount of love. Nan was always at our house everyday without fail. It was almost as if she constantly lived at our house. I fondly remember she was always there playing games with me and my friends. Like Ian, nan's sense of humour was fantastic, I would laugh with her at every single joke she made or any little physical thing she did to get a laugh. Nan was nan, and I am glad and proud to have known her and to have been her granddaughter. We would regularly take trips out as a family, often to by the sea. We had a lot of fun as a family.

I used to go horse riding with the hospital to a special riding school for the disabled to help strengthen my muscles and hand-eye coordination for me to learn how to balance myself. I was given a pony named Shandy who was adorable!

The balancing must have worked as my physiotherapist at the time was amazed how independently I could sit by myself taking into consideration my condition.

I hope you can get a sense of the normality I felt with my family along with the constant love that was always there without fail, from just reading the examples above of the regular life I had.

Despite all of the normality established above, I did have to recognise my Cerebral Palsy in school, (as it meant having support and daily physiotherapy.). I always knew that I had a disability when I was young but I didn't really know what that meant at the time. I just thought I sat down all day where everyone else stood, which can be considered a

relatively good thing from a child's point of view. It's only in later life
disability can be seen as being alien and frightening unfortunately.

My family didn't shy anything away from me in regards to my Cerebral Palsy. It's true that I didn't really have a great amount of knowledge of my condition, all I knew was I attended school with other children like me (not necessarily with the same condition as myself), but what I knew to be a typical child at the time. To be honest I didn't know that able-bodied children attended school strangely enough. I just thought children with special needs had to go to school.

Before I continue, I just want to make a little clear note. I am personally not going to identity any individual that I have had any struggles with, as I don't believe it will benefit anyone involved, including myself. I will keep anonymity, but still keeping true to reality, not for shock value, but to share my own experiences of living with a physical disability both the good and bad times in order to enhance the normality of disability in general. I just want to make this clear.

Younger Years

There was a period of time in the early years when my mum and dad did send me to preschool with a mixture of both able-bodied and special needs children. All I remember is the awful experience I had. From a young age, I was absolutely terrified of everything in existence. You name it, I was terrified of it, whether it be talking dolls (which I'm still uneasy about if I'm honest) or just a bit of fluff on the carpet, everything made me scared.

All I can remember is each morning screaming, crying in absolute fear to my mum in the buggy not wanting to go to the preschool. The child minder would act sweet and innocent to my mum, as soon as my mum left, the child minder's personality would change. Instead of trying to make the situation better by talking to me in a calm and caring manner, they would sit me in the corner of the dark building of where the child minders' was located, in the midst of my crying and tell me that I wasn't leaving the chair until I stopped crying. Being physically disabled, I was unable to move from the hard, wooden chair. All I could do was look at this one small window at the top of the wall crying for mum to come back and get me. They would take me from said chair just in time for my mum to come back at the end of the morning and say to her that I had been crying ever since she left without there being a reason. Being so young, I couldn't tell mum what was happening properly. I just told mum that I didn't want to go there anymore. This would happen every single day without fail.

It was decided quite quickly that a minibus would come to pick me up instead. It just heightened the fear I had. I'd see the dreaded sight of the bus. The panic would set in almost to the point where I felt like I couldn't breathe. My mum eventually gave in and stopped me going to the preschool. To her horror, a few years later, one of the additional workers explained to my mum everything that had happened. She still apologises for the experience I suffered. It's not her fault, she only did what she thought was right at the time, I don't blame her in any sense. It did make me develop trust issues moving forward however, in later life especially.

Much later from those horrific days of childcare, I started nursery school. Looking back now, I was treated honestly a bit babyish for my age, as if I was still one year old - not five years old at the time, all because I was seen as 'disabled ', (being mostly in the eyes of the hospital, alongside the health care sector as a whole.) This nursery school I used to

Younger Years

attend was a 'Special Education Centre' alongside other children with special needs, some with more severe conditions than me. I can imagine that this is why I think my potential wasn't fully realised. Having to attend a place that catered for a stereotypical version of a disabled person regardless of ability, of course there was going to be a form of patronisation hidden throughout the school. Disability at the time was referred to be a sad thing, that every disabled person needed to be treated with kid gloves. If a disabled child did show signs of intelligence, that didn't matter. Nobody was prepared for this scenario. These two words did not connect years ago, so it was ignored and played out as if an intelligent disabled child didn't exist. Special needs schools at this time just grouped us together under a general disability label and we were all treated the same. We were not allowed to be individuals, to explore our potential, everything seemed to be catered for one type of disability, and so, other, more able special needs pupils had to go along with this for a number of years. Special needs schools had the equipment to assist and support disability on a physical basis however there was no opportunity for disabled pupils to reach their full potential with any mainstream education. There was more emphasis placed on the physical needs of the pupils rather than any possible educational needs.

There were chickens within the school grounds which (if we had time) mum would make sure we passed everyday so that I could say hello and goodbye to them.
It's strange, but I personally don't mind disability being referred to as 'special needs' in some regards. It does depend however on the context. In my mind, we all have needs that can be considered 'special' (from an individual's personal perspective) to help assist us on our own personal journey through life. This is what I refer the term 'special needs' as being for me. Yes, I could be considered as being naive by others, but from all the (again that word) misconceptions that I have personally had to go through, you may be more understanding of why I feel this way today.

I did have other normal childhood experiences growing up. Going to Brownies was one, with able-bodied children. I was able to participate in all activities regardless of my physical appearance. I sat on the floor with the other children, but with an adult sitting behind just in case I fell back and ended up lying sprawled on the floor! It was an

Younger Years

amazing experience for me to have been given the opportunity; looking back I was allowed to be who I actually am for a couple of hours. It was nice to be able to forget about hospital appointments, splints to correct my feet (they hurt like hell as they rubbed on the side of my ankle constantly,), social workers, support workers, physiotherapy, etc. I could wear trainers and dress like everyone else, blending in! You don't know how much that meant. People take their lives for granted, but for a person with a disability, it means the world especially knowing the difficulties that my condition can bring, not just in a physical sense, but an emotional and mental sense also. Other, more 'disabled friendly' opportunities in the form of clubs after school became available. This club wasn't what I wanted or needed. I wanted to be and feel normal, but this club never offered any sense of normality. All activities catered for the more severely disabled, (simplistic and limited.), not for children like me. This was to include everyone, but because of this, no friendships were made. It's a fantastic idea, but in reality, it's less so for a milder form of disability and in some cases is demeaning for that milder group as it makes a disabled child without a learning disability feel less important. We don't need that, every form of disability should be catered for, not just a small amount.

There was a new family member by the time I was at Brownies, in the form of my eldest niece, Alisha, courtesy of Leanne and her then partner. Being relatively close in age, she became my best friend. We did absolutely everything together, like I did with Ian, but Alisha was a girl so we did the typical girly things together especially as we got older, pamper days were a particular favourite of mine! She came on holiday with us, she virtually lived in our house every single weekend. She was just there, sleeping in my bedroom with me, then when Ian moved out to live with my now sister-in- law Ceri many years later, Ian's old bedroom became her weekend bedroom. That's how much time we spent together. She did enquire about my disability when she became aware of it, but I explained that I just couldn't walk and needed a wheelchair to help me to move, but I'm still me, everything else works and she was accepting of that, for which I appreciated.

The special needs school I attended for a few years eventually closed down in 1998, so we were transferred to different schools. The local education authority decided to mix mainstream and special needs. This was great! It was a step in the right direction for equality and diversity. Special needs children were allowed to mix with other 'regular' children, whereas years before, the idea of this would have been alien. Special needs and able-bodied children would never have mixed. Before this, able-bodied people were considered as having a higher level of intelligence than special needs people. The disabled were seen as being stupid, for want of a better term. I know this as I personally have had to go through this throughout the course of my life. A certain type of education was taught for the disabled, whereas it seemed that the greater opportunities were only offered to the able-bodied as they were seen as more knowledgeable at the time. The disabled were offered an alternative type of education let's say, without any of the 'perks' of a normal education that offered the better opportunities for the future.

Everyone has some form of knowledge, able-bodied or otherwise. Giving special needs children the same level of opportunities was ahead of its time.

I was transferred to a mainstream infants school for the first time ever in Johnstown. It was a bit daunting as I didn't know what I was supposed to do, I knew it was a mainstream school as mum told me about it and how it was slightly different to the school life that I was used to. I was a bit nervous, I'll admit. However from the get go, I loved it! I made able-bodied friends who I continued to be friends with into the juniors. I still was in the special needs class of the school, but I had friends that actually wanted me and didn't see me as disabled. It was a bit alien for me to be honest to come into a mainstream school and see the advantages of a much more advanced curriculum rather than the one I was used to in my previous special needs school in Wrexham. I think from that point onwards, I thrived and wanted to be much more than I was perceived to be. Instantly, I was recognised as having a much higher level of intelligence than what the condition allowed. I think that I just didn't want to lose the new life I discovered and worked my hardest to maintain that life. I was finally given the opportunity to have the life I didn't really know that I could have. I grabbed it with both hands, and never let go from that point on.

I must have made an impression with my teachers at the time for when it came time to go to the junior school, I was automatically put into the mainstream classes within the mainstream school with all of the friends I made in infants. It felt amazing. Nothing like this had ever happened before. I didn't really understand the reason why to be honest, I didn't really know that my knowledge was on a different level of a disabled person at the time. I was still under the disability team throughout junior school and had to have a support worker come with me to the class everyday just in case I needed personal care, but to go from a special needs school to where I ended up, looking back, it was wonderful! I'm glad the teachers saw my potential and pushed it so much that I was able to achieve opportunities that I may not have been able to. I consider myself lucky.

Having special needs, doesn't mean stupidity in any sense. I'm proof of that.

This term of 'special needs' however can also have negative thoughts, again, by the lack of education of the subject disability as a whole. Mistaking inability of some people for weakness, and therefore giving us pity, not allowing us to try. How are we going to learn if we don't try?

The thing is, disability doesn't always mean inability. We can probably do a lot, given the chance, but in order to find out, we need that chance. Yes, I do agree that some people who have a condition in some way do need extra help depending on the severity of the person's condition, but to put us all under the same umbrella is discrimination. It needs to be realised as fact that there are different levels of disability and that disability cannot be just be bundled together. Action needs to be taken sooner rather than later to recognise the differences of each disability and the abilities of each person with a disability, mental or physical. It is awful that conditions are just seen as one big thing without actually talking to the person in question to actually find out their capabilities. Believe me, I have been here myself, and it's a thing I had to go through, never mind have to accept.

This is the main reason for writing a book like this, just to give some idea on disability and hopefully change the idea of the subject and end any further myths. I am personally fed up of the constant lack of knowledge of disability and hopefully I really just want to create a better understanding to enhance equality for everyone.

Younger Years

I know I'm repeating myself in the book, it is important however that the message of equality is not lost. Yes, this could just be based upon my own personal experience and views on disability, but the fact is, if I have experienced negativity, so have many others in the same position as me. We need to look deeper at all of the avenues and keep hitting the point that people with disabilities are normal everyday human beings, contrary to popular belief. We just sometimes need assistance in order to live a normal existence. This assistance shouldn't detract in any way of what a disabled person ultimately craves, which is independence in some way.

I don't really just want to make this book about me. I'm using my own life and some of the struggles I have faced as a guide in a way, to focus on the key issues that are being raised more or less unknowingly by everyday people towards the disabled, whether it be physical or mental, and I want to use my capabilities in writing to finally speak up and give a voice to others who feel they can't, as they maybe scared of ridicule or just because their disability means they are unable to for some reason.

Chapter 4
Primary to Secondary School

Any person, young or old with special needs has the right to live a full and decent life. It doesn't matter if they have a disability or not, everyone has the right to live a full life filled with normality, dignity and acceptance. I personally experienced a relatively normal life, with dignity and acceptance up until the age of eleven.

Junior school was normal. I was able to prove to everyone, (myself included), that I was able to achieve goals that others could, without much difficulty. Activities and clubs within the school helped me to believe in myself, improving my confidence and understanding that I could be so much more than my condition, something of which I have carried on believing to this day. I went swimming, participated in sports days (even though I came last in every race!) Ian put a stop to that later on during other sports days by running with me as if his life depended on it whilst I was in my manual wheelchair to the finish line! It felt great to actually come first for a change! I even went to trampoline club in junior school with the help of support workers. They would get on the trampoline with me and sit behind me whilst another support worker would jump up and down on the trampoline in order to encourage movement of my muscles. I tried for choir too in junior school but I think my voice wasn't that good as the teachers soon stuck me in sewing club instead! All that hard work with singing practice in my early years with nan on that tape recorder was for nothing! At least I can stitch something if and when I need to! There was one thing I really wanted to do when I was in primary school, and I have no idea why I wanted to do this. I wanted to play the violin. I remember being taken out of lessons and being given a violin to try. I was so excited! I tried it, and the teachers said that they would look at ways to make it easier for me to hold the violin and took it away. I never saw that violin again. This didn't lower my confidence at the time however. I had a good circle of friends that came with me from infants. I felt like one of the normal children. My disability didn't come into question, so much so that I was seen as cool by the others for being a little different but still being who I was. I'll always remember the very last day of junior school, the final year had a leaving party with a barbecue. It was fun, but also bittersweet as this was the very last time I was going to see all the friends I made many years before. I still have photographs from that day with all my friends that I had taken before we all went to different schools.

However, change comes to the best of us. It was a major change for me to go from that happy little school life that I was so comfortable with and attached to, to a different, more intense (in more ways than one) school life. You know when I said that any person regardless of ability should be allowed to have a fulfilled and dignified life? Well this idea completely failed when I went to high school. I wasn't prepared for the intense level of bullying and backlash that came with the brand new environment. Just the level of loneliness and abandonment I felt from those five years alone, I couldn't understand it at first. It was immediate too, there was no preparation for it. Naively, I just thought my popularity in junior school would carry on into high school. I soon learnt that image is everything in secondary school. My appearance I think was the driving force for the bullying.

Absolutely none of these feelings surfaced in primary school, however, my own disability became the elephant in the room in high school. I felt under-appreciated for who I actually was at the time. The support workers made everything worse as they were there to just do their job and that was it. No friendship developed in high school with any support worker I had, or any pupil. The popularity I had in primary school was significantly different to say the least. Although at one point I did naively believe that one support worker in particular wanted a friendship to develop as they suddenly decided to be over friendly. They came to the house after school once, then phoned mum once every so often for a chat. I just thought I finally found some normality. Then, one day, I heard my support worker chat to another support worker about me and my family when the school disabled toilet door was closed. She was clearly talking about me and my family's personal life to the other support worker, thinking that I couldn't hear what was being said. I don't actually know how they thought I couldn't hear everything, but I let this continue for a while until I felt I'd gathered enough evidence to share with mum. After mum got involved, those 'chats' outside the toilet door mysteriously stopped. This only added to my growing insecurities.

Another support worker I had, questioned everything I did. Their attitude was constantly negative towards me, making me feel useless and having me doubt my own abilities and life choices.

I felt like there was a stigma to who I was at the time. Something of which I never truly expected or experienced before. I only wanted to make friends again and get the sense of normality that I felt in primary school back. My disability, I felt at the time put up a barrier from that normality that I so desperately needed. I just seemed to have unintentionally taken on that alien viewpoint again from my early nursery school days.

I always stuck to the rules throughout school life, even more so during high school. No make-up, no highlighted hair, I always wore my school jumper, (even in Summer when the temperatures were well into the mid twenties!) no skirts, just trousers, tie and top button on my shirt always fastened correctly, etc. It wasn't worth taking the risk, my life at this point was hellish as it was. I didn't want to give anyone ammunition. Other students broke the rules. Not me, never me.

The only saving grace I had was again Ian. He saw the difficult time I was going through, so he would now and again take me out after school for tea, the cinema or shopping to Manchester. Just the two of us. It was extremely therapeutic to say the least. I needed something to reaffirm my normality and this was it. A few hours away from the constant undermining of who I was and another taste of the regular life I previously led and became accustomed to before high school.

Bullying is horrible no matter how it is presented and can be a harmful thing to deal with anyway, but having special needs puts a whole new unwanted spin on the actual concept and subsequent action of bullying. I had to endure this often during my time at high school. I'm not detailing the bullying I endured word for word or action by action for personal reasons mainly, but just imagine a then teenager suffering from body image issues, like many a normal teenager does but with a physical disability mixed in. Add to that verbal abuse and constant isolation, and you get just a taste of what was happening during that time. I am not seeking sympathy in any regard, I accept that children can be cruel, sometimes unintentionally as they may not know how to deal with a situation that they have not experienced before, but I'm just making it known that exclusion in any sense should not be tolerated regardless of your personal appearance. The bullying however never turned physical and I consider myself lucky enough in this regard not to have endured this type of abuse, but the verbal negatively and actions in terms of isolation were enough to tip the balance of my own perception of myself. Being laughed at and pointed at was the biggest negative part I had to endure, along with having a door being slammed in my face intentionally. It was horrible.

I did make two friends, however. They seemed nice enough and seemed to want to spend time with me. I let the walls come down a bit as I thought they were genuine in their supposed friendship. Only later, in the last year of college did I realise one of them wanted to spend time with me just to help them with their work. Despite my popularity, my grades were high, and I think that this person took note and took advantage. The friendship I thought I had was one-sided, it was only to benefit them. What's the expression? You see things through rose-tinted glasses? I think this was the case for me.

This was the time I tried different things, never breaking the rules mind, just as an attempt to fit in. I didn't like who I was anymore, sorry to say, but felt ashamed of what I was. Never in my lifetime did I have the need to feel this way. Up until this point, I had never felt judged or felt the need to compare myself with others. I started straightening my naturally curly hair, something which I still do everyday. Experimenting with clothes that fitted in with the rest of the students on the weekends, gone were the pretty flowery dresses in pink and headbands I used to wear, for jeans and a casual jumper or t-shirt along with more fashionable shoes. Everything you could think of I tried in order just to try and get someone to like me. Why would I want to follow the crowd? Why wasn't I proud to be who I was? Why did I want superficial people like this in my life? Simple. To feel normal, ironically.

I was normal, I am normal, but to go from day to day with the constant negativity put on your mental health, a 'regular' person would be bound to doubt themselves, let alone a person with special needs. To put it bluntly, I wasn't thinking about myself anymore, only how I could regain the whole popularity vibe I had going on in primary school and if that meant selling myself short, then I was prepared to be a fake version of myself.

Basically, I lost control of my own ability to accept my disability for a five year period. I'm not proud of it but if that's the only environment that you're subjected to, then you are a puppet to said environment and do almost anything to fit in. You have no choice. It's quite easy to see that this is where my mental health deteriorated quite significantly, from what I once was, a happy, popular child with all prospects ahead, to a shy, timid person who was questioning her own existence.

I was made a Prefect, but because I was seen as disabled again and nothing more, and wasn't allowed to be with the other pupils in the school yard at lunch or any other break time for that matter. On a side note, I wasn't included in any sports days because of my disability; a bit of a difference from primary school to secondary school. I was made to just sit and watch others. It was demeaning to say the least. Every lunchtime without fail, I was made to attend the Disability Unit, which was just a room to hold all disabled pupils for an hour to be 'looked after' by the support workers. I could never do what I wanted. This barrier that the school built between the disabled and the able-bodied pupils did absolutely nothing to shatter and rectify the myth that all disabled people need to be 'looked after'. This method just added to the stigmatisation of the disabled. My grades didn't count for anything, they never told a different story of my abilities. That wasn't of interest. I was disabled and had to be treated as disabled outside of the classroom. This was the only interest.

A SENCO is an abbreviation for a Special Educational Needs Coordinator, who raises educational achievements by making provisions for pupils within a school with special needs. I found this definition through research, I don't actually know what it means if I'm totally honest. What I think it means is these people are there to provide disabled pupils with what they need to be able to learn easily with things like equipment etc.

There was a SENCO within the Disability Unit in secondary school whose responsibility it was to make every disabled pupil feel normal within the school and provide essential equipment and understanding for a wonderful secondary school experience, (remember this, as it will come to some importance later). The first SENCO that was at the school did everything in their power to put the job description into practice. After the initial SENCO retired in my third year at the school, the new

SENCO that was sent in their replacement did absolutely nothing to help.

I was made Prefect of the Disability Unit within the school. Why would a Disability Unit need a Prefect? Who knows?! My only guess is that the teachers and support workers felt the need to give me something to do. I didn't really need to do much - just not let any able-bodied students into the unit without a 'pass'. No able-bodied student would ever want to be associated with the unit let alone barge inside the unit! Ultimately and unsurprisingly this role led to further ridicule. The concept of needing a Prefect in a disability unit is ridiculous and beyond me in all honesty. It looked good on a CV though, so I didn't complain!

My personality in secondary school changed quite a bit from what I once was, so much so I was forced to do two things whether I wanted to or not. The first thing was 'group', where you would go, (sometimes missing lessons,) into the school chapel and basically it was like an uneducated form of counselling. You would have to tell everyone about your personal life, the good and the bad (mainly bad) to teachers and other pupils that attended to 'accept it' and 'move on.' There are many issues regarding this attitude and handling of such a situation. One major thing is no anonymity. Everyone knew where I was going and when. There was absolutely no discretion in any sense of the word. This ultimately obviously added to the isolation I felt. Another example of this is the thought by teachers that it would 'do me good' to attend a course in another secondary school for special needs students. Why? I have no idea. I went however as it meant going from the hell I was experiencing in my own school.

This didn't lower my anxiety however. It just added to the stress that I had to endure for five years. Nobody treated me as if I had any capabilities in secondary school. Everything was just formed around my disability. It never helped during the third year on that I was the only person in a wheelchair, which just opened up that door for even more bullying. It was horrible to have an experience where the focus was just constantly based on my appearance alone. There was absolutely no opportunity to grow and become more.

It's easier for people to disregard people who have some form of disability rather than judging themselves for judging the disabled individual. What gets to me is that the majority of people never think they are doing anything wrong. That we are the problem for being disabled so it's okay to make a point of it by making sure disabled people are made to feel uncomfortable. That it's okay to make us feel like an outsider. It's never okay to do so. If you do, with intent, then you are just giving permission for hate to occur and just general discrimination, no matter what you like to believe. Only people who are small-minded allow this to happen and small minds equal small chance of acceptance.

I always wanted to go to Disneyland from an early age but as my parents weren't comfortable with the thought of flying, I never made a trip onto an aeroplane until I was twelve where I went with Ian, Leanne and a four year old Alisha. It was the best experience - and not just because I didn't have to attend secondary school for a week! (Although I will admit, that was a big part of it!) It was even better than what I could ever have imagined. We had steak and champagne and cocktails (mocktails for both Alisha and myself as we were under the legal drinking age, obviously) most nights, all courtesy of mum and dad of course! My mum and dad booked for us to go for breakfast one day whilst we were there where we could eat with the Disneyland characters. Leanne, Alisha and I knew about it, but we kept it from Ian as we didn't think he'd want to have breakfast with Mickey Mouse. . When we eventually told Ian about it, he thought it was a good idea and to be fair, he did his best to make it an incredible experience for both Alisha and myself. I remember buying a 'Pumbaa' hat from the film 'The Lion King' and wearing it all around the park from that initial day of purchase. Staff were applauding us every time I wore it! It was an amazing experience for me, one of which I look back on fondly. I could go on and on, but I won't as I don't want to bore you!

My eldest nephew Ryan was born two years later, again courtesy of Leanne and her current partner, Mark. The family was steadily growing in size. I didn't really spend much time with Ryan as a baby, but as he grew, he became a friend for a few years alongside a nephew. He was much more tolerable! This was also around the time Ian met my now sister-in-law Ceri. I remember vividly when she came to meet us, it was just my mum, myself and Bubbles after school. I tried my hardest to make a good impression for Ian's sake more than anything.

(It must have worked as she ended up marrying him a few years later and having two lovely children, my youngest niece and nephew, Rosie and Tommy).

It wasn't long before I was going with both of them for shopping trips to Manchester, or the cinema (seeing 'The Simpsons Movie' is a memory I have in particular.) and just general bonding days for both myself and Ceri. I do think that it was extremely important to Ian that he found someone who was accepting of me. Ceri is more than my sister-in-law, she's turned into my best friend in a way also because she's always helped in some way in regards to any struggles I have faced either whether it be in the past or currently, especially.

Suddenly, it came time for Ian to move out to live with Ceri. Of course I was happy for him, but after being so close for many years, I did feel a little abandoned. I was in the middle of my GCSE's, I was trying to deal with the constant bullying from school. The support I had from him for years was suddenly gone. It was a major change to come to terms with on a personal level at the time on a mental basis, but I want to make it clear I was and still am more than happy for both him and Ceri as they now have a lovely little family which I consider myself to be a part of. It was just a shock for me to come to terms with at that time.

I still had Bubbles however, who was a little older by this point, but even though he was a small dog, he was a sense of comfort during that dark period in my life. He was like my comfort blanket and strangely, my very own personal counsellor. Yes he was a dog, but I used to vent to him often, he would lie next to me in bed and just generally give me the love I needed at the time. I felt better after talking to my dog. It sounds strange, but when you feel you can't express yourself to others, a pet who is willing to fill the void of loneliness really helps. Music, (Michael Jackson) was a must during this negative period. The sense of normality and stress relief that came with singing and (unfortunately) dancing was very cathartic for me. Music by the Jackson family still helps me to unwind and act as an anxiety buster as when I get anxious nowadays, I just put on my music, and dance and sing until I feel calmer.

During my GCSE exams, I had a battle to get what I was entitled to in terms of a separate room with an invigilator of my own, this was supposed to be an option for the disabled in order to help make an individual with some form of disability feel comfortable whist in an exam. I'm not sure if it's because of my condition or not, but I'm not good in big open areas with high ceilings as I go dizzy looking up and start shaking. The idea that this could happen was alien to the SENCO that took over from the previous and support workers alike. Your GCSEs are extremely important as they help to shape your life and allow you to go on to achieve your goals by opening up so many doors. As this entitlement was firstly denied by the SENCO, I just thought well that's it, I'm not going to be able to achieve what I want as won't be able to concentrate in that big gym hall. I just gave up, until Ceri got involved. She's a teacher in another secondary school, so she knows a thing or two about what students are entitled to. Ceri helped me to revise, especially English - as this is the subject she teaches herself and she also has an interest in history which was extremely helpful. I will always be extremely grateful for her help during this time in my life.

Both my mum and Ceri fought tooth and nail to get me what I needed in order for me to achieve my dreams in a comfortable environment. The SENCO hated to have been proved wrong, but I personally didn't really care. By this point, I was sick of the constant denial that I was subjected to and was glad to have one small win on those people. Without mum and Ceri, I don't think I would've been able to go to college and onto university without their involvement. I am grateful to them both as they jointly helped me achieve what I have and I honestly don't think I'd be where I am today (in part) without them both.

Prom was something that I felt I couldn't attend. Why would I want to be subjected to that? Nobody bothered with me during that period, I just had visions of being left alone throughout that night, to add to my ever increasing sense of self-loathing, so I didn't attend prom.

Eventually leaving such a negative place came as a massive relief. I remember that last day of secondary school fondly with a smile, just because I was ecstatic to finally leave! I had just literally finished my last GCSE exam and mum and Ian came to pick me up. I couldn't get in Ian's car quick enough! I said my goodbyes, acting sad, but feeling absolutely amazing inside. Ian put me in the back of the car, closed the door and drove away from the school for the very last time. I let out a big sigh as I felt the relief of finally leaving such an awful place. The feeling washed over me. Finally, I was free from the prison, both metaphorically and physically.

This was my personal experience of the secondary school, that's not to say that it may have changed over the years since, and maybe more of an equal atmosphere now with equal opportunities for everyone regardless of ability.

About two years ago, there was a secondary school reunion which I was invited to which was a shock. At the same time, a pupil who attended the school at the same time as me strangely enough got in touch with me. It was quite odd as they never really spoke to me in secondary school and all of a sudden, they were in constant contact. You may believe that it may have been an innocent thing, that said person may have matured in personality to gain a deeper understanding of my special needs and were just trying to make amends with ulterior motives whatsoever. I don't in any way dispute this.

The way I was treated for those five years made me quite suspicious about the sudden interaction however. Yes, I could have been more involved in the conversations, as it may have been that the person finally realised their actions made me feel worthless and ashamed of myself for five years, but like I said, I still wanted to remain on guard just in case, (for my own mental health if nothing else). I decided to protect myself from any possible backlash. I felt stronger being able to do so. This person kept in touch for a few months, asking if I was going to the reunion, and asking about my life now. I did try to brag myself up a bit to be honest. Those people back in the day disregarded me at every turn, so I wanted to give myself some credit for my achievements, and to let them know that special needs people can have a relatively normal life the same as able-bodied people in my own subtle way. There was a point where I mustered the courage to say that because of the treatment I faced at the hands of those people during secondary school, my mental health did suffer as a result. The person did apologise for their past behaviour which made me gain some control back along with a sense of closure. All of a sudden, however, almost immediately, that contact stopped. That communication broke down. This just proved in my mind just the arrogance of said individual and all of the others. Basically I feel, knowing what it was like in the past, that they were fishing for information about me. Why, for what reason? I'm not sure. People work in mysterious ways.

There was a turning point for me though in having that experience. I finally managed to tell this person how their treatment of me and all of the others contributed negatively on my mental health. This was the only thing that I got out of the conversations. So I do want to thank this person for finally giving me the opportunity to tell you how all of the negativity affected me. You have given me a sense of control back that I initially lost because of you and the others. For this, I am thankful. Although, this is the only thing I am thankful for. I never attended the reunion. I didn't want to after what happened during my conversations with the individual and also why would I subject myself willingly to that popularity contest again? I made up an excuse and haven't heard from anyone in that school since. I am also extremely grateful for that.

Chapter 5
Summer of Milestones

Freedom is a concept of individuality. Basically freedom means different things for different people. What it meant for me in the summer of 2009 was self - growth, milestones and independence, which I felt was denied for five years of my life.

During the summer of 2009, a lot of things happened. I left the school that knocked my confidence, I had my GCSE results, I went back to Cardiff for a fortnight for physiotherapy from Bobath, I was starting college in the September, and just the most important and exciting thing for me, I finally managed to get tickets to see Michael Jackson in the O2 Arena in London. The tickets were a leaving school present, (and what a gift!) Things were finally taking a turn for the better. I felt free again. My life was restarting, I felt back in control of my life and it felt amazing!

There was a bit of an issue with my fortnight placement at Bobath this time though. The centre offered me the place in order to enhance my independence, because by this stage in my life my needs were changing as I was getting older, so they were looking at ways for me to do everyday tasks that were more suited to a young adult. The sessions were for me to be able to live as independently as possible. I was excited to go back to Bobath. This new life for me was on the horizon and I just couldn't wait to get started. It was the healthcare sector, namely the Health Board, who refused to fund the placement. Bobath itself agreed to fund the placement themselves as they argued that they had already offered the placement and chose to keep their promise. Bobath is a charity, and for them to fund my placement themselves after being denied by the healthcare sector, was truly incredible and I thank them for giving me that opportunity when they so easily could have chose not to fund the placement. I am honoured to think that they saw me as that important, not to let it slip away. So I did attend my fortnight placement in Cardiff, and I loved just being able to learn new skills to enhance my life for the future. I hold a special place in my heart for Bobath as I don't think they get the credit they wholeheartedly deserve for seeing the potential of individuals with special needs and working hard for the person to realise that potential, giving them self worth and

Summer of Milestones

encouragement to be the best version of themselves moving forward, rather than just being ridiculed for who you are on the outside. Bobath breaks barriers. They certainly achieved this with me. I wish all places were as positive (without being patronising) as Bobath is. Maybe then, this world may be more accepting of special needs people. This is just my own personal opinion however.

I was in Cardiff when I received my GCSE results through text. Ian and Ceri kindly went to school to pick them up for me. I was nervous all day. Eventually Ian text over the results. I did better than I expected. You see, when you have to go somewhere where you feel belittled because of your disability and attack your confidence every single day, you start to doubt yourself. From this point however, I got back some self confidence that I had lost along the way.

The twenty fifth of June that summer was a date I will never forget. Obtaining tickets to see Michael Jackson was a dream come true. The music alone helped me get through secondary school, calming my anxiety and depression quite often. I was going to see Michael Jackson with dad, Leanne, Ian and Alisha. I was super excited! I remember the day before, most of my family, (including Ceri's family) came to see 'Thriller Live!' – (a Michael Jackson tribute show). We were going before I saw the real thing to build up the excitement, something to hype me up before going to London a month later.

I am a major Michael Jackson fan as I have already mentioned. Some people may call it an obsession, but I do not care what others think. If it's what makes me happy and forget about any troubles, then it is brilliant in my book - both in a metaphorical and also a physical sense of the word!) It was great however just to spend time with the family and I was grateful for the experience after so many years of loneliness. Trying to buy tickets was really a celebration of leaving high school - basically it was a leaving present. I was so ecstatic to learn that I was actually seeing Michael Jackson that you can imagine my grief when he passed away. It may sound ridiculous but I felt as if a part of me passed away when Michael Jackson died. After all of those years of helping me through during that dark period of my life, suddenly I felt another part of my identity disappeared, that security was automatically gone. Michael Jackson was, and still is, a considerable part of my life. That night was just horrible. That's the only way I can describe it, just horrible. Mum took Bubbles out for a walk that night, I was at home watching TV and also on my laptop (which nan had bought for me), just playing around on it. I think I was still on cloud nine with seeing 'Thriller Live!' the night before. Alisha was also staying the night. Mum came back and asked if she could watch the news. I changed the channel, then I heard. It was reported that Michael Jackson had suffered a heart attack and was in hospital. I just wanted him to be okay, I didn't care about the show, that was irrelevant - it sounds stupid now, but when the anxiety attacks start because of where you may be, and one of the tools that help is music and if something happens that threatens that security then it's like your whole world is being put in jeopardy. Then the news said that Michael Jackson passed away. I couldn't breathe. I started hyperventilating, screaming and crying. That one constant in my life that I could turn to was suddenly gone. The funny thing was all of the family started calling the house as soon as it came on the news just to see how I was! I unintentionally woke Alisha up, Leanne and Mark came running around, nan was phoning. Basically all I wanted was to sit on my own, on the laptop and see if the news was true, all the while trying to hold back tears. I tried the official website, but that was down, the news was just saying the same thing. I just broke down. Mark came in to see if he could help. I just threw my laptop at him! I still have the crack in the laptop to this day! I just wanted one minute to see if it was true. I just needed my own space. Alisha came into the living room eventually. She knew how to handle the situation, being only nine years old at the time, she was amazing. She just sat down and consoled me. I eventually calmed down but this was the beginning of the countless setbacks I had since secondary school.

My dream is to one day go to America and visit every single thing associated with the Jackson family, just basically do a Jackson family tour around, seeing where they grew up, venues where they performed, visit Neverland, etc. Just do absolutely everything associated with the Jackson family.

The idea of college was a daunting thing for me. After high school, I didn't know what I was heading to. All of these negative thoughts that I may be ridiculed again for my appearance and that thought of loneliness was awful. Ceri tried to put everything into perspective by saying that if they didn't like me for me, then they were not worth bothering about.

Summer of Milestones

The thing was, I didn't want to have to go through the same thing again. I wouldn't be able to cope. Basically I didn't know what I was heading to, and that absolutely terrified me.

Chapter 6
Higher Education Part 1 - College

Working hard for an end goal, whatever your ability, should always be commended. If you can dream it, you sure can do it. I've learnt through the years that it doesn't matter what other people may think, what matters is what you think. Believing in yourself is what counts.

Starting college for the first time felt like a lamb being led to slaughter. The fear of bullying made the anxiety I felt worse. I did want to go to college as I wanted to further my education so I could potentially have some prospects in life. I wanted to prove to the bullies that I was more than what they thought I was. I'm glad I went.

The difference between college and secondary school was significantly better. From the GCSE results I got, I was automatically put into the higher level of the course without having to complete the foundation year first. My confidence came back a bit and I felt happier for the first time in years. The level of independence that came with such a place was clear. All of that negativity in secondary school

College

was replaced with the sense of normality, freedom and independence, but the sense of peace within my own mind was wonderful. The support workers were very down to earth, I got together with past friends from my hospital days from when I was a child, as well as making new friends. I could go into town during my free time and lunchtime. Going out with friends for lunch was an incredible experience for me, from sitting alone at lunchtime in high school to going with friends for lunch was a sudden welcomed change. I remember that I would come home every single day giggling from what had happened during the day, it was a major difference to secondary school, where I would come home feeling miserable every single day. It was amazing how my life changed for the better. Everyone noticed the difference in my personality, going from a shy, teenager with a lack of self- confidence to now becoming a carefree, happy individual. The transformation was incredible. I even felt included and confident enough to want and have an eighteenth birthday party, which was something that I'd never thought I would ever want due to my lack of confidence in secondary school. My family pulled out all of the stops to give me a wonderful night. This was an absolutely amazing experience for me as friends from primary school came which was wonderful to see them again, alongside friends from college and all of the support workers came too. For the first time in years I felt, happy, confident and included. I felt like I mattered. I just felt better both physically and mentally all-round from what I once was.

I often think back to those years, especially the first year, wishing I had a time machine to go back and relive those days of freedom. I will always think of this time as special.

One major thing that happened during this time was having the opportunity to go to my very first proper concert with Ian. Mum and dad came along too for the ride up to Cardiff, but didn't come into the stadium to watch the show. It was a Michael Jackson tribute concert with most of the Jackson family performing, which was absolutely amazing! Basically seeing most of the family I'd known of since the age of three, physically within the same place was mind blowing to me. I turned into a stereotypical fan for at least two hours of my life. Screaming, crying, dancing, singing, I just couldn't believe that it was actually happening. To go with Ian too was great as I felt at the time we were bonding again in a way. I did make Ian dress the part too to match up with myself. I lent him one of my many fedoras, I bought him a Michael Jackson t-shirt (that was two sizes too big for him) and even gave him a pair of Michael Jackson socks. I know he was embarrassed to wear these things, but it didn't matter how embarrassed he felt, he did it for me, which I wholeheartedly appreciated!

That sense of abandonment that I felt when Ian left home, temporarily left me whilst in that stadium. I felt as if I had my brother back, my support for so many years was suddenly back, for a little while at least, and we were sharing this overwhelming experience, at least for me, together, which was just fantastic. I will always cherish that memory.

There were things however that did affect me during that period in my life.

Firstly my nan had a fall in her home which led to her having care towards the last years of her life. This was the start of her deterioration although it wasn't to the extent that it became a few years later. She still came with us for day trips, etc., but now instead of her walking stick, she used a wheelchair. This was the only difference. Her personality was still the same, she just couldn't walk too far anymore.

Remember when I said about a friend from secondary school that I thought was genuine but turned out not to be? I found this out in the last year of college. I'm going to be extremely careful how I say this as I haven't had the conversation with the individuals involved before and I would rather not cause any friction for either person, or myself. All I'll say is that I had two friends in college, one I had known for many years and the other since secondary school.

Quite suddenly, they started to become friends with each other, which was fine, but I felt excluded for the most part. If they arranged to meet, more than likely it wouldn't involve me, which again is fine but considering that I was friends with the two of them, one whom I had known years before college, that feeling of abandonment I felt when Ian left home returned with a vengeance. All it seemed that I was good for was getting my so- called friend through college as they constantly asked me to do their work or help them in some way. I remember that one day it was getting too much so I snapped. The person asked for help and without thinking I just turned to them and shouted all over the class

College

"Why don't you try and sort the problem yourself?" That was a turning point for me as I wouldn't have said boo to a ghost in high school. I had finally found my voice again, and to be honest, it felt absolutely wonderful! It was a shock to the person as they wouldn't have expected that from me either. I was always the timid one in high school and they knew it and I think took advantage of my vulnerability for their own personal gains.

The other person used to copy me all of the time. I tried so hard to get back who I was after secondary school, after years of bullying because of my disability, I just wanted to start afresh and try to ignore my previous existence. It must have had an impact on this particular person as from the beginning, the person literally copied my life that I rebuilt. It started gradually, but as time went on, it became clear that this person was trying to turn into a version of myself. Everything I did for myself to try and make people see me and not just my condition, this person tried to copy to the last detail. It was quite strange to say the least.

The thing was, I needed to do this for myself, just to get me to a point where I felt comfortable in my own skin again, after being treated as an outsider for so long because of my disability. I would have taken it as a compliment if only they would have spoken to me about it first before doing anything. I felt like I had a bit of a battle just to keep my new identity . It's definitely what I didn't want or need.

These two individuals made my final year in college more difficult on a personal level. From that point onwards, I cut those two individuals out of my life for good.

Apart from those things, I did have a fantastic and fulfilled experience in college. We went to the cinema sometimes from the college, and day trips at the end of term. Once to Wigan for a barbecue, and a few of us (me included) went to the tutors house for tea and cake later! Alton Towers is a favourite memory to look back on from college. I had so much fun that day. We went on the Ghost House ride and basically at the end of the ride, we were just about to exit when I got myself stuck in between the seat and the safety bar! To make matters worse the carriage started to move again! The support workers were running at each side; trying their best to help me before I disappeared back into the darkness! All of my friends were laughing as I was panicking but also having fun! It is

College

the truth, you don't know what you have until it's gone. If you are lucky enough in this life to have something that you truly love on a daily basis, never take it for granted, enjoy it and get everything out of it that you possibly can. You cannot know if another opportunity will ever be available again. I will never forget those days for as long as I live. The whole experience offered me so much more than what I was hoping for, friends, inclusion, equality, independence and most importantly, freedom. Those days were, to put it in a word, epic. I often wish that I could be transported back to those days as everything seemed easier back then somehow.

I completed my three year ICT course with the final result of DMM (DISTINCTION MERIT MERIT) which gave me the grades I needed to go onto university to do the graphic design course I wanted. I was genuinely sad to leave college, which was a major difference to my feelings of leaving high school. I genuinely didn't want to leave. College gave me some identity and dignity that I lost in previous years, but if I wanted my dream job, moving on was inevitable. Those days in college were the happiest I've ever been since my happy days at primary school. I look back on it fondly. I miss absolutely everything about it.

Chapter 7
Higher Education Part 2 - University

Nothing in life ever comes easy. If you want something bad enough, you have to always work for it. You get out of life what you put in. Nothing is handed to you on a silver platter.

It can be significantly more difficult in a way for a person with special needs to want to better themselves in the eyes of society, not because of the negative ideas that a word like 'disabled' can conjure up in the minds of the uneducated, but because it may be difficult to understand the idea of higher education for the disabled and for it then to be taken seriously. Never let the narrow minded individuals of this world make you doubt your abilities. If you want something bad enough, just go for it!

Going to university was a bit of an easier thing for me as my experience in college gave me the confidence to do so. Again, because of the final grades that I had from college, I was able to skip the foundation level of the course I enrolled on which just added to my self-confidence. A few other students from college followed onto the course I enrolled on so I didn't feel totally alone making this next big move in my life. I did enjoy university, but I personally didn't really have that level of freedom I had in college. The work was more intense and took more priority over everything else in my life. Everything you did, even in the years before the final year also counted towards and whether you graduated or not depended on it. It was fine, I'm glad I went to university but because I had to put in so much of my time and effort, the actual sense of freedom was gone. Also the lack of disabled facilities within the university was absolutely disgusting and I felt it difficult to study properly. Saying that, I am extremely grateful for the experience. Nobody treated me any different from anyone else which was fantastic and something I desperately needed to continue. What I meant by 'feeling my freedom was gone' was the amount of work and deadlines that came with it. The actual reality of university quickly set in. I never really had time to think or do anything else.

University

The facilities for special needs students were non-existent. There was no disabled seating areas in the lab or classrooms, the disabled toilets were just standard everyday toilets with a disability sign stuck outside of the doors. Basically the university didn't cater for disabled students. There were lifts dotted around the campus but this level of facilities were very different from the facilities in college where every need was met. I remember having an exam once in university that lasted six hours. I had to sit, bent over this little desk on a computer which hurt my back. I was in agony for a couple of weeks after it. In hindsight, I should have spoken up about it all, becoming an ambassador for other disabled students, but I had so much to deal with as it was in terms of the workload, adding this on top, would just be overwhelming to say the least. I believed that I was just one person; who was actually going to listen to me? Who was going to take me seriously? Mum and myself did have to bring in a social worker just to alter a toilet wall by knocking it down so that I could use it when I needed to without difficulty. This however was hopeless, as they only knocked half of the wall down due to (again) budget cuts. The entire purpose for a disabled accessible toilet is for space. Space is needed in a disabled toilet for a person with special needs to easily use without too much difficulty, to get a wheelchair in, maybe use a hoist, have grab rails, but still have enough room for a disabled person and maybe a support worker or two (depending on the severity of the person's condition) to help the person use the actual toilet. The disabled accessible toilets in the university I went to were just standard public toilets just with a disabled sticker stuck on the door. When the university did get money, it was spent on state-of-the-art computers, painting jobs etc. Nothing for what mattered which was providing a comfortable, independent experience for ALL students. It was disgusting.

Recently, I have seen TV adverts promoting the university. This is fine, but I can imagine that the budget spent on the adverts could have been put to better use into buying equipment for disabled students. The university is just luring potential special needs students with a false version of the university. I'm not completely sure if any disabled friendly alterations have been added, I personally don't think the university would have thought about the lack of disability facilities or equipment. If it is still the same as it was from when I was there, it definitely needs to change.

University

I did have support workers but basically they were there to take lecture notes for me. Nothing else really. They weren't there to help in any other way in the course, they weren't allowed to. For the first year anyway. It became a little easier (course wise) during the final third year as I did have a support worker who was willing to help me with my dissertation. Stress relief was the main thing they did. Writing a dissertation is probably the most stressful thing I've ever had to do, just the amount of work that comes with it along with a deadline looming is enough to stress anyone, so I am grateful for having a support worker who gave me a calm, constant attitude.

There were four life changing things that happened during my time at university, both good and bad. I'm going to write them in the order that they happened.
The first thing was in my first year of university. Bubbles suddenly passed away. My little companion that I had for fifteen years was suddenly gone. I couldn't take it in that I wouldn't see my little pumpkin again. Looking back, the signs were obviously there that Bubbles wasn't fully well at the time he died. He had to have heart tablets a year before. Basically he had a small heart attack a year

before he died so the vet gave heart tablets just to prolong his life a little. I knew that the end was coming at some point but I think that I just couldn't believe the fact that Bubbles may not be here. I couldn't imagine my life without him. I think that I just put this fact to the back of my mind and just acted as if it wasn't true. If I were to let that awful idea linger in my mind, my mental health would get worse as the constant worry would just overwhelm me until it actually happened.

Mum came into my room to tell me that morning that Bubbles had died. I was devastated. It didn't seem true. I felt like I was still dreaming. I was going to wake up and Bubbles would be on my bed waking me up as he always did. I was in a daze. The night before, I was sat on my beanbag chair just watching TV when Bubbles just unexpectedly walked over to where I was and lay next to me. Looking back I guess it was his way of saying goodbye. Mum never told me how Bubbles died, she just said that he went peacefully. That's all I could ask for - just to know he never suffered was a comfort. It did hurt emotionally and still does to this day however.

University

After Michael Jackson passed away, all my focus was on the Jackson family. The concert I went to with Ian made me want to see them again. Having the opportunity to meet them was just on another level! My twenty-first birthday was coming up and The Jacksons were going on tour. I had to get tickets somehow! Eventually we managed to buy tickets. Mum, dad, Leanne, Mark and Alisha were all coming with me. What I didn't expect was the surprise of the meet and greet that mum also booked! Leanne came with me into the meet and greet. I was so nervous that I didn't speak a lot whilst heading to the venue in Manchester. My heart was racing.

I had a lecture that morning I had to go to in university but all I could think about was what was happening later that day. I couldn't concentrate on anything else.

Basically we were taken into the venue's lobby as soon as we were allowed to from the VIP queue. We didn't know where we were. We only knew that we were in the back of the building. I wasn't able to speak. I was telling myself not to freak out when I saw them as it wouldn't be fair to them or myself. I didn't want to ruin it. I didn't want The Jacksons to notice that I was nervous. I wanted the meeting to be perfect. I was shaking though.

All of a sudden I heard one of their songs. To be honest because I was in my own world at this point, I didn't really take notice that much. When I heard one of the Jacksons songs, I don't know why, but I thought it was the band practising before the show. Then I hear Leanne's voice, "I don't know where we are!" It was mum on the phone outside in the regular queue. She was worried because we were a long time. That music was Leanne's ringtone, not the band. Suddenly without warning, The Jacksons came into the room. Instead of feeling nervous, this calmness washed over me. The Jacksons were only feet from where I was and other fans were crying as they met them, but miraculously I never did! I honestly have no clue why, but I'm glad that I didn't end up a wreck! Eventually it came my turn to meet them, Leanne and I were the last ones to meet them. Leanne just pushed me towards The Jacksons and let me go! I had to quickly put my hands on the wheels of my manual chair in case I ran them over! They were sweet! So much so that the show was delayed by about ten minutes because they ran over on time in the meet and greet speaking to Leanne and I.

University

It came time for the show to start. Leanne was excited to see that she was in the front row with me. I didn't have the heart to tell her otherwise. Leanne isn't the quietest of people. Don't get me wrong, I love her, but her and Ian are quite noticeably different personality wise. I'm more like Ian, we're quiet, but have a sense of humour. Leanne on the other hand is completely the opposite. She's quite loud to be honest. So when it came to the show, I was glad mum told her she'd be sitting with her, my dad and Mark when the show was on. You might think it's alright to be loud in a place like a concert but when the screaming and shouting is constantly down your ear however, it becomes a whole different story! Alisha sat with me throughout that show, and she had the same personality as Ian and myself, so that meant I could enjoy myself without having a headache in the process. The show was amazing! I was dancing and singing throughout, being on the front row added to the experience as The Jacksons were interacting with me - Michael Jackson's brothers were actually giving me the time of day! When it came to the end of the show, they were throwing things out to the audience and one of them had a towel, of which they were using throughout the show. I could see them hesitantly pacing back and forth on stage. Suddenly, the towel came hurtling at me! I was shaking! I was actually given something by the people I've been a fan of most of my life. It was a fantastic moment I will never forget as long as I live. That show was an amazing, and incredible experience; something that I will always remember until the day I die. I never could imagine that something like this would ever happen. I was in awe throughout.

In the August of this year, Ian and Ceri welcomed their first born, Rosie, into the world. I remember them coming round one day for me to be able to hold her properly. I always lie on the sofa if I'm holding babies as it helps me control any spasms that I may have if sitting in my wheelchair and giving me proper back support in order to hold a baby. It was absolutely lovely to have yet another addition to the family. I was extremely pleased for Ian as he could finally have a family of his very own and I knew Rosie was going to be extremely lucky having a dad such as Ian giving her all the unconditional love and support she needs in life as he did so with me. Rosie was a sweet little baby, and as she has grown into a strong willed, independent and above all caring girl, my love for

University

her has grown alongside her. I'm so very proud she's my niece.

During my final year in university, the stress of everything came to a head. My dissertation deadline was looming, other work had to be completed and there were doubts among some people about whether I'd pass my course and graduate, which added to the stress. When you go through something as stressful as university - especially as a person with special needs, what you don't need is anyone doubting your abilities. Encouragement is always key. Nan showed me this in abundance during my time at university, especially during my third year. By this time, nan was bed bound. Carers were coming into her home more frequently to provide care. Alisha was good as she used to look after nan quite a bit at this stage in her life. We used to go and take turns sitting with nan when her memory started to decline. I do remember Leanne and myself being at nan's, sitting with her talking just to keep her memory active. All of a sudden, nan said I'll just go make a cup of tea and went to stand up. I had to grab nan's arm whilst Leanne stood up and tried to keep her seated. She wasn't as mobile as she once was and with her deterioration of her memory, we didn't want her to have another fall.

It was heart-breaking to see my nan like this, her wonderful personality was disappearing before all of our eyes. I used to sit with nan after university, laptop on my knee so I could continue working along with keeping nan company and giving mum a break. It was tiring, but it felt nice being able to spend time with nan after a long day of lectures. Nan actually helped me with my dissertation. I asked would she be in a documentary about disability, talking about how she felt now having care and demonstrating how her equipment worked and explaining her own experiences having to have something which she didn't need in her early years. The documentary was hilarious to say the least!

Because I'm uncomfortable speaking on camera as I don't really like my voice on video recordings - I sound completely different in my mind to what a video records - I asked both mum and Alisha to help, interviewing people mainly. Alisha did nans interview which was, well, a bit cringe worthy! Alisha asked nan a question on her mobility, and with pride, nan said "I can't move around as well as I used to!" with a head nod! I had to stop filming as

University

I couldn't breathe properly, I was laughing so much! She demonstrated how her rise and recline chair worked at the time. She was moaning of aches and pains, so I had to dub over some happy music in the edit to try and disguise how she was feeling. You can still tell she was complaining though from the look on her face! How the examiners took that documentary seriously enough to give me my final grade is beyond me!

Even then, I think that the idea of my dissertation, in part, was to challenge people's thoughts on disability; basically questioning the necessity of some equipment and whether it helps or hinders how people see us.

As the months went by, nan's health deteriorated quite fast. Her memory became worse and she wasn't fully herself. It was tough to take on a personal level but I bottled everything up both for her and my family's sake. It did take a toll mentally, even if I wasn't aware of it at the time. Then everything came to a head one morning. I was supposed to go into university for a catch up on my progress with my dissertation with my personal tutor. I woke up like every other morning, called mum on the phone to say that I was ready to get up as I need her help to do so.

When mum answered she explained that an ambulance had been called for Nan as she'd had a bad night. Alisha had slept the night in my room, so I woke her up to explain to her. Alisha helped me out of bed and I emailed my personal tutor to explain the situation and that I couldn't make that day so needed to reschedule, which they were completely fine with thankfully. After a while, dad picked both Alisha and myself up to go to the hospital. Nothing was said in the car. I knew it was the end as we went into a family room. All of my cousins, uncle Alfie and auntie Christine were there alongside Ian and Leanne. As Rosie was a tiny baby, Ceri stayed at home with her but was on call for updates on nan. Mark and Ryan soon followed. You could hear a pin drop. Nobody said anything. Mum explained that it didn't look good and Alisha just started crying. Strangely, I didn't, I went numb. I didn't speak all that day. I was just waiting and waiting for the inevitable to happen. I remember one of my cousins came and hugged me. There was nothing there. I wasn't there mentally. I just sat in the family room all day staring into space. Leanne asked if I wanted to go see nan. I said that I didn't want to. Not because I didn't love nan, of course I did. I just didn't want potentially the last memory I had was nan lying in a hospital bed unaware of anything. That wasn't who nan was. I wanted to remember the happy days. I didn't want any of those memories taken away. I stayed in the family room all day just in the corner in that daze just like I had with both Michael Jackson and Bubbles when they died. It came to ten o'clock at night and mum forced me to go home with her, dad and Alisha to get some sleep. I didn't want to go home. I knew what was coming. Leanne and my cousin stayed with nan and the plan was to go back in the morning. Obviously, the plan never came to fruition. I just lay awake in the dark. The phone rang at about one in the morning. It was Leanne. Need I say more? Mum, dad and Leanne came home around half an hour later to tell Alisha and myself the dreaded news. I broke down. Everything and everyone I held so dear at that point was suddenly taken away. I felt empty. The university was brilliant, they gave me compassionate leave leading up to and on the day of nan's funeral, with extra time to work on my dissertation. I remember I was also working with a group of friends on an end of course presentation to determine my final grade. They were also brilliant in telling me to concentrate on the family and the funeral, and they would carry on and help me catch up as and when I felt able to continue.

That time was like a whirlwind, everything happened so quickly on the lead up to the funeral. I'd never been to a funeral before as I was too young to go to any before nans. I just had this overwhelming sense of dread. I didn't know how I was going to react to everything.

I woke up on the morning of nan's funeral quite ready for what potentially was going to happen. As nan liked the colour green, I wore some green jewellery, with a dress of mine she had always liked, grey, with a black netted flower design and my hair in a plait as she often would say to me that she liked my hair better when I was younger before I started straightening it. I guess it was just my little tribute to nan and it gave me comfort in doing so. Everything was okay (ish) until the hearse arrived. When I saw that, it made it real. I remember Ceri was by my side that entire day. She helped me get through it as best she could. Consoling me and just being literally a shoulder to cry on. I'll never forget what she did. After everything, I wanted to go home early from the wake. I went back home with

University

Alisha and we remembered all of the good times we'd had with nan.

I was going through a rough patch in university at one point, I was basically questioning my abilities. I remember visiting nan one night after university, she could instantly tell something was wrong, even though I tried my hardest to hide my feelings. After much coaxing, I explained to her how I felt. She sat up in her bed, pointed her finger at me and said "You aren't going to give up on this, you're working too hard to drop everything now. You are nearly there. If you don't want to do it for yourself, do it for me. If you do, I'll be at your graduation. " This was the only time nan was serious with me about anything, we used to joke around and to see her become serious, was a surprise. I continued working on my university degree with that encouragement ringing in my mind. I worked day and night just to get it done, for nan more than anything. She was my inspiration to carry on and I wanted to make her proud.

After submitting everything I finally had the grade of a 2:2 on my degree course of Creative Media Computing, (a posh way of saying graphic design,) and I was going to graduation.

That graduation day was bittersweet. I was ecstatic that I was getting the reward I worked so hard for, but upset that nan wasn't there to witness it. Her help and guidance made this happen after all.

Granddad Irving was there, though, extremely proud. He actually thought I graduated in science as my degree level was a BSc (Bachelor of Science,) I never did correct him! Basically again I was there in a physical sense but mentally, I was somewhere else entirely. I was glad to get home. I hate being the centre of attention. I always have. I like to blend into the background. Nan not being there hit me hard. I wanted her to see that all the hard work had paid off. That said, however, I knew I had accomplished the one thing she had asked of me and because of this, I did feel a sense of comfort and pride. I had honoured my nan's wishes.

Chapter 8
Grief

There are different ways grief can affect a person. The actual mourning process can take years to actually hit a person. Everyone is different in their reactions. Some people laugh, some people cry, others become angry, or distant and some can develop mental health issues, depending on the person.

I think for a while after losing the things in my life that gave me purpose, happiness and guidance, I became distant and basically I just became worse. I had a two month period after finishing my course at university and before I graduated when the grief began, subtle at first, but it became a part of me soon after finishing my degree. That encouragement I had had from nan that spurred me on to finishing the course was gone. I put all of my energy into that encouragement so when I actually stopped, when the course was completed, the grief consumed me. I had nothing else to focus on.

I went out in the garden one morning and I just froze. I saw an empty space on the decking where nan used to sit. I just had to turn around and go back inside where I just sobbed. Everything just hit me. Losing so many in a short space of time just got to me. I think my time in high school was also in that grief. I now believe that I was grieving for the loss of myself too. My life as I had known it for so many years was gone. I realised that I was an empty shell of who I was. I tried for so many years to bury my grief to try to get back to how I used to be. In the end I was just a false version of myself. Acting happy on the outside, but inside, I was torn apart.

I don't like being the centre of attention as I have already said, so I think the mask I put on myself would help, or so I believed at the time. I used to go out and see family, acting happy, which I became quite good at.

I became dependant on chocolate as it became my coping mechanism. Whenever I felt down, I'd eat a chocolate to give me a sudden burst of energy. That would numb the pain for a while and when the energy eventually wore away, I'd eat another and another until the burst of energy was so much within me the constant agonising pain disappeared

Grief

for the rest of the day. I understand now that it was a sticking plaster to hide who I had become in order to enhance my 'happiness'.

Nan was there for us all, either playing games, making jokes, line dancing to keep us entertained, or telling war stories from when she was little. Whatever we did, wherever we went, nan was there. Not to have her there anymore, I do believe that this was the beginning of us all trying to find some sort of new way to live. How could we though, without the one woman who was our whole world?

We do still involve nan in things, keeping her memory alive by always speaking about the good and funny times each of us shared with her.

Mum, Ian, Ceri, Alisha and myself have this thing about feathers and robins. If we see a single feather anywhere we believe it is someone who has passed. For me it's either nan or Bubbles. I can't tell you how many times a single feather has appeared out of nowhere since losing so many loved ones. The other night for example, I was writing the portion of this book about nan dying, and I went into my home office to check everything and lock up for the night. A single white feather was in the middle of the room. Another feather was at the bottom of my bed one morning, exactly where Bubbles used to sleep at night, and a feather on the back seat of our car (nan's seat) was found one day. Most of the jewellery I wear these days are feather related. I have a feather necklace, feather earrings and ear cuff, feather pendants, a feather ring for my finger etc. It may sound ridiculous to someone on the outside looking in, but this belief on a personal level gives me comfort. Anything that gives you comfort when you experience a close loss should never be ridiculed. Don't be ashamed or embarrassed. Believe what you want to believe in, if it gives you the comfort and the strength to carry on and fight another day, it's the best. It's the only way to carry on in my opinion.

I did have a few keepsakes that belonged to nan after she passed away, the necklace that she always wore, a ring she wore, and the metal tea set she first taught me how to make a cup of tea with. That's all that I wanted and I treasure them always with fond memories.

Death seemed to come in a set of three quite literally after nan. Auntie Christine, auntie Julie and granddad Irving. I'm not going to discuss too much

Grief

about both of my auntie's passing away as I don't think it's fair on my dad, cousins and uncle. All I will say is that their sudden deaths came as a major shock and massive blow for our entire family and we miss them everyday.

Granddad Irving passing away came just one year after nan's death in 2015. He became ill with a suspected heart attack but didn't tell anyone for a week, by this point, he was in a bad way. I remember being in my bedroom when the phone rang to say that granddad Irving had been rushed to hospital. Mum, dad, Leanne and (I think) Alisha, but I'm not too sure, went to the hospital. The majority of my dad's side of the family were in the corridor of the hospital ward waiting to go in. Dad and auntie Julie went in and after about ten minutes, dad came out and said granddad Irving wanted to see me. I'm not good at those types of situations, I get so nervous and worried about what may greet me, (that's why I never saw nan during those final few hours,) Leanne came in with me to see granddad Irving. All I knew at this point was that granddad Irving was ill, I didn't really know what caused his illness, whether it would be the last time I'd see him, I just didn't know what to expect.

I thought that if he's asking for me, he should be okay, comparing the situation to nan. When we went into the room, granddad Irving was sat up in the bed but the amount of machines that were hooked up was unbelievable to see. He was a bit breathless too when he spoke, but I tried my best to keep his spirits up and for everything to seem normal. Inside it felt like deja vu, just like nan when she was bed bound in her home, I did my very best to hide my emotions. I never spent that much time with granddad Irving growing up, he was there and I did go to see him from time to time but I guess it was just one of those things where nan was always the main grandparent I'd see everyday. I do remember he kept birds in cages in the 'parlour room' as he called it. I'd hear these birds chirping constantly when I used to visit him. As time went on, granddad Irving did become stronger, to everyone's surprise as we were told basically he didn't have long. That again hit me like a ton of bricks. The hospital moved granddad Irving to a standard ward from the ICU, where he began to thrive, so much so, he was eventually then moved again to the rehabilitation unit of the hospital for physiotherapy in order for him to live independently again at home. Everything was put in place, (stair lift, rise and recline chair etc.) when

Grief

(again) suddenly granddad Irving deteriorated quite significantly to what he'd become. That was a shock.

I remember the very last time I saw granddad. Mum, dad, Leanne, Alisha, auntie Julie along with granddad Irving's sister, auntie Pauline were in the private room. Leanne took me outside to fully explain the situation so I was fully prepared for the inevitable this time. Obviously I was upset but I personally think granddad Irving was oblivious of his deterioration as he was sat in bed, reading the newspaper. It was a strange situation to be in, we all knew what was happening, but we kept quiet for granddad Irving's sake.

Eventually the inevitable did happen. Dad was at the hospital with auntie Julie and auntie Pauline. I was at home in my room, playing music, probably as a distraction. I think mum had a phone call to tell her the news from dad, where she came to tell me. I knew it was coming, but again I wasn't prepared for it. I lost two of my grandparents in the space of a year. Granddad Irving came to nan's funeral; now we were preparing for his. I turned my music off and just started cleaning my room. I think the anxiety that built up just came pouring out at that moment and I needed something to focus on.

Mum and dad went to tell Ian and Ceri the dreadful news. However, it was bittersweet as they had some news of their own. They were expecting again. This time it was Tommy. Mum phoned me to tell me Ian and Ceri's news but I personally didn't take it in that much - understandably - as granddad Irving had just passed away that morning.

On the night Tommy was born, I had arranged to go with Ian to see the new 'Star Wars' film. I'd pre-booked the special disabled access box in the cinema. Suddenly Ian phoned mum to say that Ceri had gone into labour. I was disappointed that Ian wouldn't be coming to see 'Star Wars', but extremely excited for another niece or nephew. I ended up taking Ryan to see the film instead. We went to see both Ceri and Tommy the next day in the hospital before they went home. Tommy was so cute, and still is! He's growing up with a cheeky, and funny personality, just like Ian. I love Tommy as he always brings a smile to my face even if I'm feeling low. He's caring and funny without even knowing it. He's great, to put it in a nutshell! Again as with Rosie, I'm proud to be Tommy's auntie.

Grief

It was a bit of a roller coaster of emotions during this time in my life. Everyone was suddenly leaving me, but in their absence, a new life was brought into the world in the shape of Tommy.

Chapter 9
Working with CP

Getting a job and keeping that job for a 'normal' person is just a standard part of life. Getting a job and keeping that job for a person with a condition or special needs is another story altogether. It's almost impossible for employers to take a person with a disability seriously, which isn't acceptable, nor should it be allowed in today's world, but it does keep happening. I don't understand why, with everyone now becoming more accepting of other everyday things, race, equality, gender etc., being able and allowed to work, why can't disabled people? Everyone just sees disability as this negative thing. We're living in the twenty-first century, yet attitudes are still backwards on this subject. I'm not an expert but it seems to me that because the disabled are entitled to benefits, we should just shut up and be pleased with our 'cushy' lives. This attitude desperately needs to change. As I said in chapter two, disabled people are more likely to take less time off work than the 'average normal' person. We want to work and will do everything we can to keep that job (if it comes, that is), and prove to everyone that we are just as, if not more, capable than the next able-bodied person. We shouldn't have to prove anything really nowadays though; supposedly we live in a world with equal rights and opportunities. Not for the disabled we don't. Let me tell you, if a person with special needs has the want and desire to work, and has the ability to do so, why should we have to always just accept this old fashioned idea of what being disabled really means? It's not right. It's disgusting and it's a form of discrimination at the end of the day.

Society never wants to be seen as being in any way shape or form discriminatory towards others, it's a dirty word, it's not them, it's the next person who thinks like that. People are always passing the blame. Society is accepting and tolerant, it's not them, they've moved on to accept everything and everyone, who they are and what they do, - the world has come a long way from what it was. But put a disabled person in the mix, and people just jump on the bandwagon and say we're too fragile. Maybe not in words, but their actions and body language say differently. It's true, actions, do speak louder than words, none more so than when the disabled are the topic of conversation.

The world of work is guilty of this, I've been there, I've had it happen to me, it's horrible, I know. Most employers do change their minds on hiring someone for a job once the disability card is laid out on the table, and if the employer does manage to look past the disability issue, then it's almost always going to be the elephant in the room. I have experienced this in my working life.

When searching and applying for a job, I have always tried to be as honest about my Cerebral Palsy as much as possible. Explaining that I use a wheelchair for mobility but basically that's it. My mind still works. This, however, didn't matter to most employers I've had the misfortune to meet.

It doesn't seem right if a person works hard all through their education, (if they have a condition or not,), and hopefully gets a good job at the end of it which then doesn't happen because of something they cannot control. It's not right whichever way you look at it. A person's self- esteem is gone once this happens, their mental health may suffer too as a result. Again, I know this because I've been there, and if I'm honest, I still suffer with low self-esteem and my mental health to this day, although I've got a bit of a hold of it now thanks to medication and

Working with CP

online CBT, (I'll talk about that later). That's not the point; neither I, or anyone else in my position should be allowed to have their self-esteem knocked or their mental health become an issue. It's not fair. It's all because of the backwards thinking of people that this happens. It's unacceptable and it ends now. Not tomorrow, next week, next month, next year, NOW. This backwards thinking has happened to me. It's not just employers who are guilty of this, but my favourite thing, the healthcare sector too is guilty of not giving the disabled a proper chance of employment.

I have had to take jobs on a voluntary basis throughout my working life due to a lack of paid employment opportunities. Actually finding any sort of paid work is practically non-existent. Why should we be penalised for wanting a normal life that includes a normal paid job?

Again, I consider this to be a form of discrimination. I understand that some people are uncomfortable with disability but I am calling for change to this attitude.

It's almost as if I don't deserve all the normal things in life that an able-bodied person has, even down to my financial status in a working environment, even though I fought tooth and nail for some normality, my life is still seen as nothing more than my CP. It's horrible to have to deal with day in, day out, just to have this label constantly hanging above your head reminding you that you aren't as good as others, something like that will play on your mental health. As I've said now for what it seems like the millionth time, we are the same as everyone else and should be treated as such in ALL aspects of life. You cannot pick and choose what a special needs person deserves. It's not right. It's not your choice. It's ours. If we want to earn a wage, and we are capable, we should be allowed to do so without being penalised for having a disability. If we are qualified and produce work of high quality, we should be rewarded for our work just like everyone else in society.

I went through three voluntary jobs before I finally found somewhere that accepts me for me, regardless of my physical appearance. I've had permission to write about my current job from my employers. I am so grateful to them to be given an opportunity to be able to do so.

Working with CP

I will start from the beginning talking about the struggles I had to face before I got something I deserve. I won't be mentioning names however as I haven't had permission from past employers to do so. Having a condition means having some form of support in order to help with living as independently as possible. The line between independence and overall metaphorical suffocation can become blurred when talking about this, however.

I've had to have a support worker throughout my life since around infant school for personal needs really, or helping me transfer from my wheelchair when I needed to. I've never had to have a support worker for anything more than this, I can accept that I need help with these things. What I'm unable and not prepared to accept is any independence that I have being taken away. There are things I need assistance with but there are many more things that I don't.

One volunteering job I had after university was for a charity. My initial role was marketing, which basically meant that I was in charge of their social media, advertising events, looking for news stories to put on social media etc. which was fine. It was one of my first tastes of working life and I gave it my all.

In terms of the actual job, it was great for a while, I made friends with work colleagues and the work was constant which was fantastic. Everything seemed fine for a while. Charity meetings were being held frequently of which I was a part of, taking members on day trips, having training days etc. It was great. I even had the opportunity to do some graphic design work as they needed posters to advertise events.

This busy lifestyle however, like most things in my life, felt like it had jolted to a complete stop overnight. I ended up just having to go and man the office on my own. There were no windows in the office so all I was doing was looking at four walls by a computer, waiting for the phone to ring (if it did) , which of course I'm uncomfortable with as I become tongue tied, my mouth dries up, I start shaking, my heart races and i cannot get any words out. It's a horrible experience for me being on the phone. This is why I lean toward texting, emailing or face to face. Phoning is not high on the list of preferences. I managed to do it however, God knows how, but I managed it somehow.

Working with CP

I remember three times where my feelings didn't count for anything; two events and one awards ceremony. I like to be organised and help out wherever possible, it's just in my nature but the charity took advantage and I wasn't shown any respect for my efforts. I went above and beyond what they asked of me. For one event, I was asked to go around town and leave posters in shops etc. advertising the event. I got my family involved, asking them take posters to their place of work and I had mum and dad taking posters everywhere for me too. I made phone calls to get prizes for the tombola. I did everything in my power to make that event a success.

The other event was the 'grand opening' of a new branch of the charity. I managed to get there with my support worker at the time. We got there early so me being me, I went to see if they needed any help in setting up. They basically shouted at me, saying that I was too early and told me to come back later. It was awful to have been treated like that, as if I didn't matter. I went to a nearby cafe until it was time for the event to begin. I was ignored by my boss at the time, as they never introduced me to any people higher in the pecking order. I was losing my confidence again.

The last time was an awards ceremony in Chester. Apparently I was going to receive an award for my efforts. Mum and dad came with me. When we got there, it wasn't disabled friendly. No disabled access ramps, and the lift was broken. Mum phoned my boss and explained the situation. They came down and just said it's arranged now and they can't rearrange the event. They then went back inside to "see if anything could be done." We just left without telling anyone. I was angry. Why book a venue with no disabled access to present an award to a disabled person? It was obvious I wasn't highly thought of.

One day I was in the office and a member of the charity came in and said that they had an appointment with one of my work colleagues. I wasn't told anything about this, to be fair I was never told anything, meetings, cancellations of events, I wasn't told anything. I rang the colleague and explained the situation. They started shouting at me basically saying that they couldn't get to the office and I'll have to deal with the situation myself. That wasn't in my job description. I calmly explained to the colleague that the person in question was at the side of me (they probably heard all of the verbal abuse) I said to the colleague that maybe I could pass the phone onto the charity member so that they could explain the situation themselves, rather than having me be the go-between. At this point, I decided to look for another job. I'd had enough.

The next volunteering job I had was for a day centre. My nan actually went there for a while and had meals on wheels from them when she wasn't physically mobile any longer. They needed someone to take care of admin, but that turned into a greater role over time as posters, signs, menus etc. were needed. I sat with the day centre members in the morning just chatting before my actual job began. It was lovely as it reminded me of being with nan. Eventually as with everything, the work died down and I was let go.

The most soul destroying volunteering job I had was working for a well-known graphic design company. I applied for the job and I was on holiday when I received an interview date. In the email I sent to begin with, I explained all about my Cerebral Palsy as I did with every job I applied for. I went for the interview with my support worker and everything seemed great. I had a start date and I was ecstatic to finally work for a company fully dedicated to graphic design. It became obvious however that the boss wasn't totally comfortable with me. On the day I was working, the boss always had a meeting in another place. They never set work for me, they didn't even talk to me. My colleagues were great. I got on with them and felt accepted in this way, I just didn't feel accepted by the person who initially gave me the job. The atmosphere was becoming worse every week, I was feeling uncomfortable. At some point however the boss did ask one of their employees to ask me if I could do a promotional video for the business, (they never asked me themselves). I planned everything for the video but I needed to run it by the boss for their input also. This never happened. There was always an excuse why they couldn't sit and look at my plans for the video.

It came to a head when I was leaving for the day.

The boss seemed very keen that day to speak with me, which was odd as they did everything they could to ignore me. I did feel better though. I felt as if I finally turned a corner. When it came time to leave, it happened.

Working with CP

The boss followed my support worker and I into the car park and said that I wouldn't be needed anymore as a colleague was going on maternity leave soon so they would have to close the business for good. Obviously this was a lie. My colleague was going on maternity leave quite soon, this was true, but, as great as they were, there was absolutely no need for the business to close completely. Other colleagues explained to me that the boss had an issue with my disability and this was the reason why they let me go. I was livid. After everything I went through to try and gain a normal life for myself, to have that cruelly ripped away because of something I can't control, was soul destroying. In no way, shape or form is it right for one human being to treat another human being like this, regardless of ability. It isn't right. I think I've made this point clear. To be fired because of a disability, something of which I have no control over, which is a part of me, (but I've always refused to let it become an obstacle,), and for it to become an issue for someone else, is just unacceptable and cruel. Any way to describe the humiliation caused by a situation such as this cannot do it justice. I would not have minded so much if there was a valid reason for letting me go but they were just uncomfortable with the fact I was in a wheelchair. I hope and pray that this does not happen to anyone else in the same position as me. It is just horrible. I was determined to not let my disability become a part of me. I am so much more than my physical appearance.

That night, I sent my CV out to every graphic design company I could find, I was just so desperate to try to prove to myself and others that my disability wasn't going to hold me back. It was the last email I sent that became my saving grace. It was a graphic design company for the motorsport industry. Designing things for motorsport (helmets, race suits etc.) along with websites, logos, car liveries etc. for clients. I sent my CV, expecting nothing back. I shut down the computer and turned off my phone after sending my application. I just wanted to go to bed after the day I had, as I felt very depressed. Quite surprisingly, I heard back the next day from the design company, and we set up meeting for the following week.

Mum and my then support worker came with me to the interview. I remember I lost my voice after having a really bad sore throat. It's just my luck, I get an interview, but can't speak!

Working with CP

When they arrived, and we all sat and talked about me joining the business, it became clear that it was a family business I was joining as my boss' mum also came to the interview. From what I understood, the business was just starting to gain momentum as it was relatively new, so they were looking for someone to join on a freelance basis to help out with design work basically. It took a while to grasp admittedly, but I started a month later from the interview, as when I applied, it was during the busy period and my boss wouldn't have time to teach me the software properly. I loved it when I started! I was quickly thrown in at the deep end, but I loved the fact that I was trusted enough to be given the opportunity to work almost instantly. I never had a clue about the motorsport industry but since starting the job in 2017, I took it upon myself to learn. I sat and learned as much as possible, watching races on TV as I didn't want to go there without knowing what it was. I was determined to do everything to keep this job as I was terrified that the same thing was going to happen again. Nothing was going to stop me. All of those previous setbacks just made me want to prove to everyone that I was worth something, despite what anyone else said. My confidence grew a little. I met my boss' dad too during this time who again didn't patronise me or belittle me, something of which was refreshing. It was quite funny however as they thought I was "posh" (their words) when I first started. Probably because of the wall I built throughout the years to try and keep my mental health in tact. I never really spoke in the beginning, I think for two reasons, partly because of all of the let downs I've experienced prior to getting my current job along with other stresses that I had to deal with that was stopping my independence. When I first started working with my employers, I had a support worker who would accompany me, but after a couple of years, when I no longer needed the support, I felt that also gave me greater independence and confidence, as I was able to go to work on my own.

When I had to let my support worker go, I found that my employers felt that I was quite independent working on my own, and it worked well.

My life was starting to get better. I had a job, which gave me a sense of purpose and a degree of independence. I was finally getting to use the skills I'd qualified in and felt valued by my employers.

This was the best I'd felt since my college days. Mental well-being can be fragile; sometimes it can be the smallest of things that can have a devastating effect and bring anxiety and depression back to the forefront.

I have had this happen to me in the form of little white lies here and there, which I initially brushed off, but the lies just kept coming and coming, and those lies then turned into promises that weren't kept. It never stopped. It started small, I remember asking a couple if they would like to come with me to a concert as I had spare tickets, they said that they couldn't as they had a prior engagement in a another city that particular weekend. This was absolutely fine with me but I saw one of them in a local restaurant the day after the concert. This broke me. They said that they were at the other end of the country all weekend and couldn't go with me, yet, there they were. I couldn't believe it. I was heart-broken that they thought it was okay to lie to my face and had absolutely no problem in doing so. I kept that experience quiet, as I didn't want confrontation and I didn't want to believe it. I know that I should have been confident enough to confront these people, but I wasn't. They still have no idea that I saw them. I do wish those people would have been honest with me about the concert as my respect and estimation of those people went down so quickly after that. Maybe the people in question didn't want to hurt my feelings, but to lie to me? A quick decline may have initially disappointed me, but the actual lie is going to stay with me forever, and that is something nobody can undo regardless of how sorry they are. The damage is already done.

If you don't want to do something with someone, just be honest and say no, your relationship with that person will always be stronger. Honesty is the best policy. My mum has always said that you have to have a good memory to be a good liar. Clearly, certain people don't understand this.

Just being continuously lied to and the constant use of empty promises does eventually affect you on a mental level. Able-bodied or otherwise, if that behaviour is non-stop, which in my experience it unfortunately was, it can cause your mental health to deteriorate. My mind just kept deteriorating with every lie and promise not kept and I just got the feeling that certain people didn't respect me as they said they did. As I've already mentioned, it's true what they say, that actions speak louder than words. I can now say in hindsight (which is a wonderful thing), that I was experiencing a form of manipulation. I couldn't see what was happening at the time as my head was clouded by these people. I was ready to defend them in any way that I could, not only to others who challenged their treatment of me but also to myself, as I didn't want to believe that people would be so cruel.

Unsurprisingly, my mental health deteriorated. To tell you the truth, I think it was a combination of several things that lowered any sense of confidence I once had and made my mental health worse. For one, I think that I allowed myself to lower walls I had built up throughout my life. This paved the way for obvious and catastrophic setbacks to happen, mainly caused by those people who thought it was okay to play mind games with me by their constant empty promises and lies. I started having panic attacks in work, but I never told my employers about this until much later. I dropped my working schedule (actually physically going to work) from once a week to once a fortnight. Sometimes during this time (when I felt that I couldn't go to work physically), I would work from home, but the work would be so far and few between most of the time, I felt as though my anxiety and depression was getting worse. I somehow developed this need to check everything in sight. Basically everything had to be a certain way otherwise I couldn't cope, the pressure would be too much to handle in my mind. I know it sounds ridiculous, but this is how my life was for so long. Any doors would have to be shut quietly and not to make any sort of banging noise, otherwise I wouldn't be able to handle it, I would be worrying about so much stuff, it's unbelievable what would actually trigger a panic attack.

The recent pandemic made everything a million times worse. We weren't allowed to do anything or see anyone which meant I wasn't able to go to work, and the work dried up as a consequence of the global lockdown. I needed to be busy, more so during this time which didn't help in the slightest.

I knew something was wrong, but my mind couldn't break free from the prison it found itself in. It was exhausting, both physically, and ironically, mentally. I absolutely hated who I became when my mental health was at rock bottom. When I was young, everyone said how fun I was, with a big smile on my face, but since everything happened later on in my life that gave way for my mental health to deteriorate, I was a shadow of my former self. I wasn't happy, I constantly argued with everyone, I worried a lot about different things that others would find silly, my sense of humour was gone, as was my sense of identity. I just didn't know who I was anymore, and I didn't like it. I can't explain the thought process that made me change so much personality wise, because I don't really know why it affected me as much as it did, and why it materialised in the way it did, but all of the negativity with grief, empty promises and lies, trying to prove my worth, bullying and every other negative thing that happened to me did affect me badly.

Sometimes I can be okay, then it just hits me out of the blue. I am a million times better now because I have started on anti-depressants and I'm currently doing online CBT (Cognitive Behavioural Therapy,) which is basically a form of counselling where they look at mental issues and encourage the person to face up to their fears. My family and friends have said that they have seen a major positive change in my personality and apparently I'm back to how I used to be when I was young. I'm a lot calmer and I'm not as panicked about things as I once was, thankfully. There is still a little more progression to be made, but I'm about ninety percent back to the person I used to be, and I love it!

At the time of my mental health deterioration, I stupidly tried my best to hide my feelings from everyone, trying to silently cope when inside my head felt ready to burst. I did go through a patch of having to complete everything A.S.A.P work wise. It was an ordeal for everyone. I knew something wasn't right but I couldn't stop. Everything I had to design was completed literally within ten minutes and that's not an exaggeration. Otherwise it would be on my mind until I finished.

The chocolate obsession continued also. My employers were feeding the obsession that made my mental health deteriorate more. I must stress this was in absolutely no way their fault. They weren't aware that this thing I had for chocolate was an inner demon that I was battling. I never told them. Maybe because I didn't want to admit it to myself that I did have a problem. It was my coping mechanism after all and I was terrified to tell people, that security blanket I had would be ripped away. It was my fault for not telling my employers. I do not blame them for this as they thought that chocolate was 'my thing', if you like. This hidden battle became my undoing.

Working with CP

Eventually I realised that the chocolate fixation was only there to hide the grief and setbacks I've faced throughout my life. Basically I'd eat chocolate to feel better, but as soon as that sugar rush would leave my body, I'd fall back into the darkness of my mind, so I'd have to have another to replace it in order for me to be 'happy' again. It was my choice; and by giving me a choice, I can now say that I have a handle on it. I eat chocolate but not to the extent I used to. I can go a couple of days without chocolate now, but if I want one, I will have one. I'm not denying myself. I've learnt how to manage it depending on what I'm feeling.

One day I was going out with mum and dad where everything just came pouring out. Basically I had a severe mental breakdown in the back of the car. We had to drive back home as I couldn't do anything. I went on my bed, screaming and sobbing. I even told my employer I couldn't work for them anymore. I think everything at that point prior to working for my boss, along with the combination of empty promises and lies from people who I thought I could trust in the past, just slowly crept in and I felt like the walls were closing in on me.

The next day, when everything eventually calmed down, I spoke to my employers about my mental health issues. They gave me time in order to get the help I so desperately needed in the form of counselling

I must admit that the concept of counselling terrified me. I had only a vague impression and didn't really know what to expect. When I started, I explained everything to the counsellor about all of the setbacks I had faced throughout my life, and they came up with the plan of me doing extra volunteering on the side of my current job. They even had a position in mind and assured me that this company had a proven track record of hiring and working with people with disabilities. This sounded perfect.

I went back home and explained this to my employers and they were extremely supportive, and my boss gave me a glowing reference.
As I was attending my counselling sessions, it became clear that something wasn't quite right.

You know the phrase that starts, if something sounds too good to be true? Even though I was told that the new business owners were extremely keen on meeting me, the proposed interview dates were pushed back all of the time; there was every excuse under the sun as to why I couldn't meet the manager.

Eventually the counsellor admitted that the job wasn't actually going to happen. They said that the job fell through as the company didn't have any disabled facilities despite the fact that they'd employed disabled people in the past. This in itself was confusing to say the least.

This setback never helped in any way with my mental health. I felt that the one person who's job it was to help, never did. The counsellor did offer me a job to work for another department and so I went for yet another interview with the person in charge of the department that I was going to do some work for. They needed someone to design the wall art for the new gym and wall art for their new office being opened by the coast.

I went for the interview and saw what needed to be done and I went away and came up with three ideas. I created the first design. They wanted it in a different style. That was fine as usually it takes a good few attempts to get something right for a person in graphic design.

This is not unusual and yet, this time I received no feedback whatsoever from the second design.

After several weeks Mum phoned and explained the situation about not having a reply. She was told the project had fallen through due to lack of funding so I was no longer needed. That was another blow. I couldn't believe what was happening. It would have been wonderful if they would have told me themselves. Instead, I just felt like there was absolutely no respect. That experience just added to the stress and pressure in my mind.

The people in these departments are supposed to be there to help people with problems and yet the way I was treated left a lot to be desired; let's just say they were very unprofessional.

We did try to complain about the 'help' I received from the entire department but we received the impression that everyone just closed ranks. Nobody seemed interested.

From the experience I had back then, somehow everything seemed so bleak, but as time has gone on, it's made me realise that I'm not the problem, the problem is society not allowing people with special needs to live as independently as they can. It is a terrible world we live in. Everyone should have the opportunity to show their abilities, regardless of their appearance.

One thing that I will say for my employers is that they have said that they see me, not the wheelchair, which is what anyone wants. A wheelchair, a walking frame and crutches are just aids to mobility , the same as a bus or a car would be to an able-bodied person to get from A to B. People should never judge us on our initial appearance. We are more determined to succeed in life. Equality is the most important thing that matters. I'm coherent and capable. I just need that chance. I'm so grateful that my boss took that chance when they so easily could have said no to my application straight out. I am not grateful however for how society as a whole has somehow managed to adopt some sort of hierarchy where the opportunities are always open to able-bodied people, when the disabled community always has to fight for the same opportunities. I'm afraid that this cycle will never end. It doesn't matter what you do to show your capabilities and worth, there will always be that barrier, that label that inevitably follows us around which stops us from living our lives because of small-minded people, unless we recognise the signs of the discrimination and change once and for all. It's terrible that we are still treated so poorly by those who think that they have the right to dictate and decide what we can and can't do. It's just upsetting. People also think that they can treat the disabled as if we are stupid, for want of a better term, by lying and promising things people have absolutely no intention on carrying out. We are human beings, we are not sub-human but we are treated like animals. The manipulation and patronisation I cannot stand either. Basically, these people need to start to rethink their ways and approach. Why should able-bodied people feel superior to disabled people? We are all the same, but also, everyone is different in their own way, and that should be celebrated, not ridiculed or taken advantage of. We shouldn't have to fight for everything. It's cruel and unnecessary if anything. It is the way in which society thinks that they have the 'upper-hand' in the way they treat the disabled that is simply awful. I think as well, this superiority complex is due to the fact of eye level. A wheelchair user is always automatically at a lower perspective compared to an able-bodied person. It could be something psychological that people automatically think that we are vulnerable, having to look down at us may turn into society looking down on us. That's the difference, and I don't think it's a difference that people are aware of, unfortunately.

At the end of the day, we just want and need to be accepted for who we are, and be given the same opportunities as everyone else. We are not there to be manipulated, controlled or even physically or mentally abused. We are not vulnerable, if anything we are stronger for our experiences, most of which I doubt that any 'normal' person in society could deal with. We don't want any special treatment however. The most important thing that a person could do is give people with special needs the chance to succeed. We don't want permission, we don't need applause or recognition for being as independent as possible, and we just require the same chances as everyone else in life. Of course this seems extreme, but I personally feel that there is an underlying and silent case of this behaviour in society, that people often mask with patronisation. It's not right. I'm absolutely sick and tired of the way people see the disabled. I'm ready for that change, I've been ready for years. I just need society to realise how discriminative they are towards people who are living with a disability. I'm done with the constant looks of sympathy, I'm done, with the prejudice, I'm done with the lies and empty promises people think that they can say to a disabled person without consequences. I'm done with it all. I'm just done.

Chapter 10
Mental Health and CP

Research says that more adults with Cerebral Palsy experience a mental health issue of some form, compared to adults without the condition. I can accept this as I personally had and still have to fight for everything which I feel that I am entitled to. I can accept that this is the case for everyone else with a different condition too, as more often than not, the same battles have occurred with others. I can guarantee you that. Everything is heightened and more difficult for a special needs person to be taken seriously, compared to other people in general society, as what you may take for granted, we have to fight for the opportunities that just comes naturally to others. I'm not in any way trying to get sympathy for us, as I've previously said, none of us need sympathy. What we do need is just equality. I'm merely saying what needs to be realised for change to finally happen.

That was my life, which is quite surreal to tell you the truth. All of that pent up tension I've had for so many years is finally out there. All of that pressure has finally been released. The amount of relief and satisfaction I now feel in doing so is too much to put into words. I do still suffer with my mental health. Some days are better than others. When the recent pandemic hit, my mental health deteriorated gradually, as did so many others in similar circumstances. I couldn't go to work, and to make it ten times worse, the amount of work slowed down to a complete halt because of the pandemic. I couldn't see family or friends, I wasn't allowed to go shopping, go to the cinema, etc. All of the things which helped me to control my mental health and give me the life that I worked day in, day out to achieve were replaced with isolation and, of course, the constant worry about the pandemic itself. When the first lockdown started the same thoughts went through my mind about all of the setbacks that have happened during my lifetime. All of the empty promises, lies, discrimination and bullying from certain people throughout the course of my life up to this point, slowly returned. I felt very depressed.

The impact of the constant empty promises and lies on top of everything else I had to face throughout my life just added to this deterioration within my own mind. This made my confidence lower again to a point where I felt undermined and unimportant to some people.

I keep my promises. I love to make people happy by any means necessary, and if I promise something to someone, I make sure that that promise is fulfilled. I cannot understand people who just promise the world but do not act on a promise. It is just cruel. I know a lot more than what people think I do. I don't like confrontation, so with every lie I have been told, I've held every single one within me, for them to slowly contribute to the deterioration of my mental health. I know its unhealthy holding every single lie within myself, but I personally would rather keep them to myself than to risk losing people who I have found that want me as a friend.

One thing that surfaced during this time of the first lockdown was one person in particular. I think it is safe to say that this individual has contributed to the deterioration of my mental health. A constant presence in my life in the form of shopping trips, concerts, days out, the loneliness that I felt when they decided to leave one day after everything we went through together, was too much. This person has their own life now. That's fine. Everyone is entitled to a life. That's what I have been saying throughout this book. I just wish that they would've thought of and involved me as much as I thought of and involved them throughout the years.

The recent pandemic made it difficult for me to see this person to begin with for obvious reasons. When the rules relaxed a bit, so you could see one person outside your household (practising social distancing guidelines of course,) I hardly ever saw the individual, which was heart-breaking as I was so close to this person in the past, to hardly ever seeing the person was just a horrible experience I had to deal with.

My parents, for personal reasons, would be reluctant to take me to some places I wanted to go and certain people would be willing to take over, which I was grateful for. These people would be willing to do things with me, but there was usually a down side in the form of arguments and misery, (started by one person in particular.). It was never a happy experience. I would buy tickets so that they would come with me but every time there would be a miserable atmosphere. There was so much negativity surrounding any event that looking back I now question why I invested so much anticipation and excitement when I should have realised that each trip would become so depressing. Sadly it's the misery I remember as much as the anticipation.

My relationships with all individuals mentioned above in this chapter is non-existent at the moment. They don't understand that my mental health has suffered, they haven't been in touch with me to find out how I'm doing. To be honest, in some ways it is a relief, not to have that constant negative niggle. I am feeling much better for releasing that pressure. Relationships are about give and take, and neither individual was appreciative of the effort I put in to keep our relationships going. I really would not have cared so much if there had been some form of gratitude. There was nothing. The relationships I have had with these people has been one sided. I am not prepared to accept this anymore. I deserve to be with people who just want to spend time with me for me.

I think the exclusion I suffered in secondary school planted the seeds that caused the deterioration of my mental health. I personally think after I left university all the setbacks I experienced with different employers, triggered that pattern of negative thinking. Then, with the onset of the pandemic and resulting lockdown my mental health developed into a more severe issue; I developed depression, OCD and anxiety all at once. I think this is a big contributing factor in the breakdown of certain relationships.

I will let you know about my anxiety, OCD and depression as I'm not ashamed of it anymore. I'm getting a little stronger each day in trying to control it through my recent course of medication and CBT. I will not however go into each issue as I do not think mental health issues can be defined as being one thing. There are a number of different things that can trigger a person's mental state. You cannot categorise mental health as one thing, just like you can't class every disability the same. I am writing about my personal experiences with mental health, covering the issues I have. It is not right to write about issues that I have no understanding of. Only the people who have other mental health issues can do that. I will not only write about my mental health struggles and how it affects my everyday life, but also how I am slowly overcoming these struggles with help.

I personally think that my mental health issues were hiding within me for years. I actually think it is a combination of my treatment as a disabled person, bullying, and the constant empty promises and lies from people who I once trusted. Basically the decline in my mental health started gradually. I had to check everything was switched off in my bedroom before I left the house. Eventually it became worse, with my computers especially. I had to check they were working four days a week, then that morphed into checking and rechecking my home office. Recently I've developed this fear of any doors in the house banging in case one of my laptops falls over, potentially breaking them. I do things in either a count of four or ten, depending on how brave I'm feeling at the time. I now have insomnia and I have to keep the TV on until I eventually drift off to sleep.

As I have already mentioned, I have got help recently with the help of anti-depressants and CBT counselling online. I've stopped checking the computers from four days a week, cutting it down to two days a week. I do check if my computer mouse is switched off in my office but only if I'm working in there. When appointments are made, I do need advance warning so that I can plan in my mind everything that I need to organise to keep things running smoothly so as to not cause me anxiety. I need to feel in control to reduce my stress levels.

I am learning to manage my mental health bit by bit. I am getting there with the support of my family along with getting some normality back that I lost due to the recent pandemic.

It's still a long journey with many ups and downs, but I can't wait for the day that I finally reach the destination. I am getting there though. Recently I have felt much better than I have done in years with the help of my incredible family and friends who never gave up on me, the ones who could actually see my distress and did absolutely everything to help me through. Being put on medication and CBT therapy is also helping a great deal. Everyone can see the positive change in me, and most importantly, I can see that change myself. Being able to put everything into perspective and having the opportunity to look at what makes me stressed, and remove most of that stress which has given me the courage and confidence to overcome my mental health issues bit by bit. I'm feeling stronger, happier and I feel proud of myself for having the determination to do so.

I do believe it all stems from the setbacks, backlash, empty promises and lies throughout my life that has contributed to my mental health deterioration. I didn't really recognise the signs back in those days as I just thought it was normal behaviour to experiment with your appearance at that age. What seems like standard behaviour can quickly escalate into something much worse.

If you are constantly belittling a person by nasty words, it is heart-breaking and does nothing to help the situation. People with mental health issues do not want to hear negative, hurtful comments. Yes, it may have been said on the spur of the moment, but those words last a lifetime to the person suffering. We need help, not ridicule. Think before you speak.

I am learning not to let the nasty, negative comments I had to experience in the past damage my own self-belief and self-worth, otherwise the individuals have won. I am not sweeping it under the carpet though as it is making me strangely stronger to prove that opinions will never hurt me, no matter how much they try.

Disabled people should not be made to feel a burden on society. Therefore if you do find people are saying nasty things about you or to you, never allow yourself to become disheartened. They are never worth your time or your headspace. Use that negativity to your advantage and become stronger with every small criticism that is said. You will become the better person overall. The disabled have the right to live independently if they so choose and if they are able, with a minimal amount of restrictions. Trying to get this across to people though is like repeatedly banging your head against a brick wall. Society should be encouraging people with special needs to live as independently as possible, instead of being treated as something that needs extra care and attention. From personal experience, I believe that all disabled people are seen as the same. We're like robots that need to be 'fixed.' Every disabled person is unable to have any form of independence. We're seen as being unintelligent, needing help constantly and just generally different from everyone else. The idea of disability scares people. If society is able to band us all together then it's like as if people can identify us as being in one group. That is more mentally acceptable for society. I am sick of being treated with kid gloves, what I personally lack physically, I sure do make up for mentally. I can imagine that other people like myself feel exactly the same. The only difference is that the rest of us sadly do not have a platform to speak our minds.

Mental Health & CP

Any book about disability is always leaned towards the negative side. However you would be hard pushed to find any book associated with any form of Cerebral Palsy. The books that do have CP as the subject matter is always referred to as 'understanding Cerebral Palsy,' I personally wouldn't mind this as everyone needs to be educated further on the subject in my personal opinion. That word 'understanding' however is always focused on the negative side of the condition. Books just seem to blanket disability as this one thing, something that is almost always focused on the disability, never the possible ability of an individual.

The 'disabled friendly' after school clubs I had to go to were just awful. All of these clubs were for the severely disabled, which was fine, but other people with special needs had to go along with the activities that were more suited to a severely disabled person. Playing pass the parcel at the age of ten was one thing these clubs did, just to give you an idea of how every single special needs individual is treated just because of what people can see. There was absolutely no room for individuality or personality. In the minds of society I believe that we are seen as stupid and the only way to communicate with us is through ridiculous patronising behaviour that belittles our potential and our confidence, which is a dangerous thing to do. Just because we are physically disabled, it does not give you the right to make an assumption on our mental capabilities. I stopped attending these clubs as I felt like I had more to offer than what was being offered to me.

We all have some level of intelligence. It's just having the opportunity to show our intelligence, that's the hard work. It's as if we don't understand anything, we are basically stupid. This is absolutely not the case. We're probably more intelligent than the rest of society put together. Think about it. We have had to learn how to live a life full of challenges and obstacles. We have had to learn to adapt in order to enhance any possible chance of a normal life, breaking barriers, just generally learning how to be us. What hasn't adapted is any sense of equality from a society. I'm getting weary now trying to get this point across, that we're just as normal as everyone else, we just need that chance to prove it. Denying any individual their right to live as independently as possible if they are so inclined, can be detrimental to a person's mental health. I'm living proof. Mental health is finally becoming increasingly important in society, but this does need more exposure to enhance understanding of the effect discrimination and inequality has on the minds of the disabled. Just because it is written in books, on the Internet, even discussed in the healthcare sector as something worrying, the truth is, disability shouldn't be made to be this sad thing, all people with a disability shouldn't be treated the same. Individuality is the most important thing.

At the end of the day, all people regardless of condition, ethnicity, religion etc. deserve the right to live. If we just take into account the abilities of each person (as everyone is good at something,) instead of always focusing on the disability, maybe then we can start to live in that just world we all like to believe we live in and make equality the most important thing and any mental health issues may stop altogether, making an individual the priority, not their so called 'imperfections.'

I've spoken about how disability is seen, but I didn't really go into any detail of the actual personal experience I had to face. If I'm out and someone is just constantly staring at me, it makes me feel uncomfortable and anxious. I wish people would just ask if they have a question about my Cerebral Palsy. I would be more than happy to answer any questions on my Cerebral Palsy as I know more about the subject than most. It would be more acceptable to do this. I personally think that the stigma of disability stops people asking questions, but think about it, staring is worse and is more unethical as it makes the disabled person feel like they have something worse wrong with them than they actually probably do.

I can't speak for everyone, but I can imagine that this is the case for everyone who is living with a disability of some degree. I am well aware of how annoying it is when someone looks at you differently as if you've just arrived from another planet in your alien spacecraft. You're perceived as inhuman almost and this should not be tolerated in any sense.

People with special needs do need this encouragement. We have been mentally and emotionally kicked down with the constant negative treatment we have to deal with on a daily basis. Enough is enough. We don't want to be labelled - I certainly don't, I've worked too hard for someone to come along and stick a disabled label on my personality. I know I'm disabled, it's obvious, but I personally don't want to be reminded of it everyday.

Mental Health & CP

I hate to have the disability label put upon me. Make no mistake, I'm proud to be who I actually am, I'm happy and I've accepted who I am, I just cannot tolerate people who think they know me just because they read about Cerebral Palsy somewhere.

We all have different levels of ability. The label just hinders any amount of ability and individuality we do have in the minds of society. We always have to fit into society's idea of what a 'disabled person' is. We cannot be true to ourselves. We cannot have dreams of being something greater than what our disabilities portray us as being. It's just not acceptable to do so. There are always barriers that disabled people have to overcome, day in, day out just to be seen as a human being.

Now is the time to rethink disability, not to discriminate but to include, offer equality and show we are able to adapt to all diversities. Only then we can have a just world free of inequality and discrimination and therefore mental health issues may in fact become a thing of the past for the disabled. That is my wish anyway.

The majority of people do not get mental health problems either. The idea of this subject is put down to being over dramatic. We are told just to deal with it. It's one of those things, you're not depressed, anxious, etc., it's just your mind playing tricks. Put up or shut up. This attitude towards mental health (like disability) needs to change also. If you suffer from mental health issues and you are constantly trying to silently cope when inside you feel like your whole world is crashing down, all because some small minded individual has told you just to "deal with it", it becomes worse, as if it's almost our fault, not society's.

I'm sick of all of this backwards thinking on these two subjects. People say they understand just to look good in front of the rest of society's backwards ideas of what the two topics actually mean. They never put in the time and effort to actually educate themselves on each subject properly. These individuals are just there for the praise and glory to be seen to be helping someone who needs help. Sadly, there's no actual understanding of the situation.

There is help out there, I've finally found it and I'm finally on the road to recovery with my mental health. I'm getting there with the help I so desperately need with counselling, support from family and friends, self care in various ways including using my breathing techniques from said counsellor, ASMR, reading, singing and dancing (in private!), my Himalayan salt lamp, and getting out with my new support worker. The healthcare sector is finally at long last sitting up and taking note of what I need. It's not ideal, given the length of time they have taken with the sudden constant intrusion of appointments, giving me an overwhelming feeling of anxiety. This was something I wasn't used to. It seems I had become 'lost' within the system, (whatever that means!), but I'm slowly coming to terms with the disruptions to my routine when appointments are made. It's a slow process but with the constant love and support from my family and work, I am getting to the point of having my own sense of self-worth back, however it is still a work in progress

Chapter 11
Deeper Understanding of Disability, Mental Health and Subsequent Treatments from a Personal Perspective

Let us look deeper into both disability and mental health as a whole and try to change some misconceptions on this subject, as I believe that disability and mental health go hand in hand.

Disability and mental health can be a daunting thing for people to deal with. People never know how to handle it when it's in front of them. It's something that someone else has to deal with – not that one individual. Burying our heads in the sand and not confronting the two subjects has a detrimental effect on a person with a condition, mental health issues, or both.

By doing this to a special needs individual, you could be allowing mental health issues to start, as you may be unintentionally giving the impression that you don't care about the person or the condition, when in fact it may be that you are

A Deeper Understanding

uncomfortable to speak to them for fear of either saying the wrong thing or in case of something happening that you alone may have to deal with.

Disability isn't a choice, it's a way of life for the individuals who have a condition. The line becomes blurred when that truth isn't fully realised. Intentional or unintentional, this behaviour needs to stop and needs to be a part of modern culture now. We are not in any way inadequate to you, we desperately need someone to take us seriously without patronising us constantly just because of our appearance. Ability shouldn't come into question. What should come into question is how people treat others who are different. Every other movement is now being recognised for the seriousness it deserves, whether it's Black Lives Matter, Black history being finally taught in mainstream curriculum in schools, gay rights, etc. Why should disability and mental health be treated any differently? There is absolutely no excuse. Now is the time for change. Everything about both subjects should be encouraged to be as important as all the other topics that are now within social consciousness.

Disability in general is described as being either a physical or mental condition that limits a person's movements, senses, or activities; a disadvantage or handicap, especially one recognised by the law. A limiting lifestyle and a disadvantage? I'm sorry but this isn't true. It's insulting that the world sees us like this. The only limitations are how people view disability and see us as one thing. By now I hope I've given you enough time to realise that we are not just one thing. We are not the label. We are humans looking for that one chance to prove to anyone who would give us that chance without any doubts or hesitation. That's all we need. That's what we deserve.

Like I said, I do consider myself somewhat lucky to have that sense of opportunity finally, even though I've had to fight every step of the way to achieve it. Others in my position aren't so lucky unfortunately.

Disability is treated as something to be handled with care, wrapping a person with special needs in cotton wool as the big bad world maybe too much for the person to handle. People with conditions are limited through the sense of the world not giving disability the chance. To push the boundaries on what disability means and to break the misconceptions. I'm going to say this again in a more clear tone. The limitations come from the world stopping our dreams so we fit into the

A Deeper Understanding

socially acceptable form of the term. Our limitations are not caused by our disability. Our limitations are caused by the human race not giving us a chance to explore our potential abilities. This paves the way for our mental health to deteriorate if we are always just put into one category.

As discussed in previous chapters, the exclusion and loneliness I faced particularly in high school was awful and as I've already explained, the realisation of this exclusion and loneliness prayed on my mind, destroying any confidence or courage I had in my early years becoming a shadow of my former happy self. It's not at all fair for any person to take away another person's sense of self, where they are questioning everything. Their abilities, their confidence, and their identity. There is absolutely no rhyme or reason for the general public to make us feel ashamed of who we are. We didn't choose to be this way, it's just the hand we were dealt either from birth or an illness or accident that we were subjected to. It's not our fault. We have learnt to adapt to our way of living, why can't you adapt your concept way of thinking and accept the differences as a normal part of life? Why is this so difficult?

A Deeper Understanding

The reason for this constant and unnecessary backwards attitude towards disability in general could be down to a superiority complex of the 'normal' individual towards the special needs person. Think about it. You consider yourself to be normal. No condition, no wheelchair, nothing that could identify you as a disabled person. You then suddenly come into contact with a disabled person. The feeling from personal experience is sympathy, but that sympathy can turn into something much worse. You quickly turn onto the unreasonable idea of being better and more superior as you are able to walk, talk, be independent and just do everything in general. I don't actually know if this happens all of the time, I'm just basing this on my own life, but from my own experiences I know this can cause a disabled person's mental health to suffer as a consequence. It's sad but true. This is my own personal experience that I'm drawing from. My own mental health has significantly deteriorated over the years and I'm still dealing with my state of mind to this day as a result of being denied most things from people (outside my family) for years. I don't really have all the answers but I'm willing to attempt to give some understanding on it from doing research on disability and mental health and the strong link between the two subjects. I have

A Deeper Understanding

told you how the discrimination due to my disability has paved the way for my mental health to suffer as a consequence in the previous chapter. It's actually quite easy to connect disability and mental health.

Mental health is a terrifying topic to speak about both on a personal level and in a general sense. It's taken me a lot of guts and soul searching to eventually muster the courage to write about these subjects that I have become somewhat of an expert on. Mental health refers to cognitive, behavioural, and emotional well-being. It's categorised as how people think, feel, and behave. Basically their overall state of mind. People sometimes use the term mental health to mean the absence of a more positive way of thinking. On a personal note, I don't think that you can just accept this as fact and leave it like that. Defining mental health can be a difficult task in itself. There are so many different things to take into consideration. It cannot be identified as just one thing. A whole host of triggers can potentially cause mental health issues. We as a society need to start looking into all of this a little deeper to gain more understanding why mental health issues happen and do our very best to end the stigmatisation of people who have to face the same battles day in day out.

A Deeper Understanding

Never be terrified to approach the subject of mental health. It took me years to actually identify my issues and confront them. I think that I was just terrified what I would have to deal with, so I found it much 'easier' to hide it for as long as I did. That attitude from society does absolutely nothing to end the 'taboo' around the subject. Talking and understanding is what is needed to stamp out the myths that mental health can bring once and for all. Talking about it openly will help all parties; the person living with the mental health issue may recognise that they need help, and the person initiating the conversation will have a clearer picture of how mental health impacts an individual. Hopefully, by doing so, this will make the world realise that their concerns and concepts of mental health, as with disability are wrong.

Some ways to make you feel more comfortable in approaching someone with a mental health condition is to be able to set some time aside from your busy schedules, stopping any distractions to let the individual talk as openly and honestly as they want without any time constraints. Let the person share as much or as little they feel comfortable to share, pushing an individual to share more, will only antagonise them and make

A Deeper Understanding

them rebuild the walls. Never self- diagnose or impose your feelings onto theirs, it would only have a negative impact if you do. Listen carefully to how they are feeling, never try to make it 'better', you cannot. Just listen. This can be the most important and impactful thing you could do, and if you feel the need to ask questions, keep them open-ended. You will only unintentionally influence their feelings if you ask closed questions. After they have shared, speak about the benefits of wellbeing. How it will help to take time out for themselves away from the struggles and frustrations that life can bring. Talk about how doing something for themselves, will ultimately improve their life in a positive manner as they will have a calmer demeanour to cope with everyday tasks much better. Most importantly, explain to them that you are there if they ever need to talk, (and mean it!) Having someone in their corner helps the person realise that there is an issue and find inner strength to confront and make it easier to manage.

Constantly blaming individuals who have a mental health issue, because you feel that they are not trying hard enough to overcome the problems they continuously face or never stepping up to a challenge, can have a detrimental effect on that person's overall mind set. They will start to realise the negatives constantly being thrown and believe that negativity as fact, creating a person with low self-esteem, so in turn, the person's expectations are lowered. People with a mental health issue never need to hear that they are the problem, it's their fault that their lives have turned into something much less desirable than they first imagined; that their lives would be so much better if they did something to reaffirm themselves.

When you suffer from a form of mental health it can be extremely difficult to think about doing anything. What we need is unconditional love, understanding and support, that's it. A sympathetic ear never goes amiss either. Stop trying to self diagnosis a person, and just listen. You don't have the answers, nobody expects you to, but just being there for someone in their hour of need can work wonders. Believe me, I speak from personal experience.

To be fair, TV has only just started to realise that mental health needs to be taken seriously and therefore they are doing their very best to highlight the topic in a positive way through campaigns. I personally do believe that this has taken centre

A Deeper Understanding

stage because of the recent pandemic. I cannot think if a stance such as this has been taken before the pandemic. There does, however, need to be more exposure alongside disability for the inclusion of everyone instead of it just being a world for the 'normal people.' Looking after our mental health can help our ability to enjoy life.

Doing this involves balancing our activities, responsibilities, and efforts to be resilient. It's not that easy to get that resilience we need on a daily basis. Day to day tasks become dreadful when mental health issues appear. The concept of doing anything can be daunting. I speak from personal experience. I feel this way quite often when I just feel like crying with the prospect of what lies ahead. I have ways to manage my mental health issues as previously discussed. I will go into more detail about the different methods I use to manage my mental health as I do feel that it's important to help others find their own personal methods. These are the methods I use. It may not work for everyone, but this is just information of what is out there to help if you feel like you need it.

Mum and dad did try their best to manage the deterioration of my mental health by themselves by taking me back to horse riding. For a while, it was great. I practised on a mechanical horse just to get me back in the swing of things, as I hadn't been horse riding for many years. I was hitting all of my targets and doing well. My confidence grew. The time eventually came to introduce me to a real horse. I was a bit nervous as animals are unpredictable but also excited for the idea of doing something I once had such joy from. The horse was brought into the arena and I put on my horse riding helmet that they gave me. I was transferred from my wheelchair onto the back of the horse. I was always taught whilst practising that I'd have to lie on the back of the horse first to be able to sit properly and get comfortable. I did as I was taught, as soon as I laid back, the horse bolted and I fell on the floor hurting myself. It shook me. The people who were there to provide safety, reassurance and support, never did. I lost my trust in these people. I did go around the arena on the horse once when the people eventually calmed it down, but I didn't enjoy it. A few weeks later, I had an email from the riding school, coming up with different options for me to be able to continue. The experience was traumatic and because that trust was gone, I decided against it.

A Deeper Understanding

To help with my insomnia, I use ASMR videos on a video sharing website. ASMR, or Autonomous Sensory Meridian Response gives a feeling of well-being along with a tingling sensation usually starting in the scalp and working it's way down the back of the neck, it's experienced by some people in response to a particular sound. ASMR is triggered using whispering, paper tearing, and scalp massage, etc. I personally use the ASMR role playing videos that involve me being placed into different types of scenarios such as a spa day treatment, hairdressing, doctor's appointment etc. For me, I find these help the most as they vary from video to video. No two types of video are the same. There are many other different types of ASMR videos that work as effectively such as soft music, or light rainfall etc., depending on your level of response to this type of relaxation.

My methods of coping with stress in everyday life have basically been sourced from my recent counselling sessions alongside some coping mechanisms I have sourced myself.

Breathing techniques are a major positive difference I've found in managing my mental health. Sitting in a quiet space and becoming aware of my surroundings through that breathing helps me on a personal level. This method takes away the stress, I use this when on my computers and things aren't working properly. Instead of shouting at the screen, I sit for a minute, gather my thoughts and then continue when I feel mentally able.

Talking therapies can help you work out how to deal with your negative thoughts and feelings and make positive changes for you to try to live a better lifestyle. Also coming up with coping strategies to help you escape the rut you have found yourself living in. These types of therapies can help individuals who are feeling distressed by difficult events in their lives as well as people who have mental health issues.

Music is an escapism that I wholeheartedly have taken as my own personal therapy for when my mental health reaches it's peak. The effects of music can be powerful as it is used to promote emotional health, help individuals cope with stress, and boost well-being. When I'm alone I turn up the volume of my music and dance and sing until the feeling of anxiety passes. It's extremely therapeutic (maybe not for the people who have to deal with this torture of my singing and dancing but to me it's

A Deeper Understanding

brilliant! I can let go of all of the stress and just do something to make me happier and calmer). It's my release.

Cooking and baking are the recent hobbies that I have discovered which has helped to decrease any anxiety I felt during the recent pandemic. I put all of my energy into it when I am in the kitchen. It really has become an enjoyable experience and I am using my design skills in a way as I have to decorate cakes, and use my imagination to see what will work.

Reading is another thing I personally do when I feel anxious. I put all of that energy into this one thing and ultimately feel better after doing so. Putting all of my focus on this one thing distracts me from my negative thoughts, replacing it with enjoyment and relaxation. I am transported into a different world whilst reading and those negative thoughts leave my mind. Although sometimes depending on the level of my mental health and how bad it is, I do find it hard to concentrate.

When my mental health isn't so bad, it's wonderful. I feel better after a good reading session. Reading is a form of escapism, shrinking all of the negative tension that a mental health issue can bring.

A Deeper Understanding

Getting lost in a good book is known to reduce stress. Research says that reading and the relaxation it can bring can be useful as you can take that relaxation and incorporate it into your everyday life.

I created a blog two years ago at the point of when this book was written, on disability and mental health, looking at how to break the stigma of both subjects, which has been very cathartic to do. It's gained some positive traction on the social media platform I use. I dip in and out of it whenever I have a chance to give others some sense of identity and some sense of help and guidance through the posts I share. To make it clear, this is in no way a plug for my account to gain more followers. I would not do that. I'm just giving tips on what is helpful to me in order to enhance my mental health more positively to help you to think of ways to help and improve your mental health.

Also, I have now started a small part-time business on Etsy, called Beautifully Designed By Sammy Jade, designing a wide range of glossy A4 posters for either a home and or an office, to keep me busy when I feel that everything has slowed down a bit, basically to stop my mind from wandering. Rosie

A Deeper Understanding

has been helping to design posters too. I've given Rosie her own sub section in Beautifully Designed By Sammy Jade, called Callista Creations. Callista is Rosie's middle name, so that is where her business name comes from. She is very environmentally conscious and studious and her posters are mainly based on her passion for the environment and education. She is very enthusiastic about her designs and I must say, everything that she designs is very impressive and I am really proud of how much she has learned and taken on board in a short space of time.

I did remove myself from one social media platform in particular in the past, as seeing others live a 'fantastic lifestyle' which was drastically different to my own was causing a deterioration in my sense of well-being. I know that most things posted on social media only show the best bits of a person's life, but it was still awful for me to see those things. This social media platform I felt just added to the stress and pressure in my mind and I was getting more depressed by the second. I'm not by any means telling you what to do as it is your choice, as I've re-joined the social media platform, but I have re-joined just to promote my Etsy small part-time business, I personally don't use the platform for any other reason, but if you are experiencing difficulties with your mental health, maybe removing yourself from the toxicity of social media could be the first step in the right direction.

I am not ashamed to say that sometimes, when the pressure builds to a point where I feel that it is just too much, I do cry. It releases some of that pressure and puts everything into perspective. Everything seems to lift a bit in my mind and as a result, I am able to cope a bit more. It is like a pressure cooker that sometimes builds up. All of the setbacks, discrimination etc. just comes to the forefront and when I do cry, the dark cloud passes for a bit. Crying is an extremely therapeutic way to remove stress or anxiety, as crying releases endorphins. These internal chemicals can help ease both physical and emotional pain. Your body may feel numb once these endorphins are released into your body. Endorphins such as oxytocin can give you a sense of calm or well- being. Like I previously said, I personally tried to do this with chocolate, until that anxiety slowly came back, and I ended up having a mental breakdown. I thought I had a handle on everything, but I never did; if you don't show your emotions, you are just prolonging the inevitable. Never be ashamed to show your emotions. It's powerful. Basically you are just releasing pressure in

A Deeper Understanding

order to give yourself more of a chance to cope with stress. Do not fall into the trap of self-denial. If you feel like crying, cry. It's better to cry and let your emotions out rather than burying feelings in the hopes of them disappearing. Those feelings never fully disappear if they are never addressed properly. You are just blocking the emotions, giving way for future struggles. Showing emotions just confirms your strengths; weakness comes from hiding your emotions. You have more ways to work issues out if you cry as you are letting out your stress. You have a clearer mind once you have finished crying, so in turn you have a clearer picture of the situation you find yourself in and you are then in an ideal position to solve a problem with a calmer attitude.

We are not limited by our own abilities, we are limited by society unwilling to give us a chance to show our abilities. This is the real disability.

Chapter 12
Conclusion

Even though the title of this chapter is the conclusion, it is in no way the end of the conversations that have been spoken about in this book. The conversations need to keep going until all stigmatisation of disability and mental health is changed to accept, understand, include, and give equal rights to a person with a disability and/or a person with a mental health issue. This is just the beginning.

What I aimed for and wanted to do with this book was to break the stigma of disability by sharing my own personal experiences living with my condition of mild Cerebral Palsy to hopefully show you regardless of ability, we are all able and entitled to live a normal life without being penalised for doing so. To get you rethink the idea of both my own condition alongside disability as a whole. I do sincerely hope that I have managed to open people's eyes to the stigma that we face on a daily basis just because we look a certain way, and hopefully managed to end any further myths and backlash because of how we look.

Conclusion

I may have made myself unpopular in writing this book about my struggles both on a personal and a generalised level, but at this point, I have literally decided to be true to myself and not hide my thoughts or feelings anymore on anything. I have suffered many years of disappointment and loneliness and having to live a lie. Pretending to cope when inside I could not. It needed to have been written in order for me to take back some control and hopefully try to help others along the way. No amount of backlash I may get from telling my truth, will compare to the backlash that I faced during my lifetime up to this point.

I definitely do not want praise for this book as this book should have been out there years before I felt the need to write it. I'm just taking it upon myself to voice what needed to be said years ago. A lot of people in the same position as me feel the same way. I can guarantee you that. I do hope that this book has given you some much needed food for thought. I hope it has given you a clearer picture on how disabled people are treated and change how you will treat us in the future. I hope this gives you a deeper understanding and education of disability to be more accepting and understanding of each disabled person that you will meet in your lifetime and give you the opportunity to treat us as equals with no patronisation whatsoever. Please do take the time to look deeper into disability as a whole to seperate the facts from the myths, just as I have in regards to CP. Other forms of disability have myths attached. We cannot just take disability as face value as it is more often not the case. What you see isn't always the truth. It's up to you to make that significant step forward for educating yourself on different forms of disability. It's not our job by rule to educate the uneducated. Put the work in yourself. You will be surprised by what you may uncover. Everyone has their own idea of what disability means, but until you have lived with a condition. I'm sorry but you are not at liberty to comment.

Going back to the Disability Equality Act of 2010, looking at my own personal experiences with secondary school and employment, it can be very easy for someone to come to the conclusion that because we have an act from parliament, then you don't need to worry about us. We're sorted. This is a misconception in itself. We're not 'sorted' at all.

Unfortunately, discrimination of disability does still happen. Even though it wasn't updated to today's

Conclusion

standards back when I went to secondary school, the act sure as hell was doing the rounds when I was in higher education and definitely when I was looking for a job. Even though I now have a job which caters for me. It's still difficult for people with special needs to be taken seriously. This definitely needs to be looked into and questions need to be answered as to why discrimination still exists for the disabled.

You may think I would be resentful of my family because they never told me about the struggles that came with my condition that I've had to fight for. They gave me a relatively normal life for so many years in my early days and a good insight into the normal lifestyle, I now know the difference in the treatment of the disabled to the general public as a whole, and am able to compare my early years of normality to reality. It has given me some confidence to spread my thoughts on disability in order to try to change the idea of what being disabled truly means, and to challenge the mind set of people to keep the sense of normality I experienced years before for others in my situation.

Something which we have not yet spoken about and I feel is more than necessary is defining the word 'normal'. This definitely needs to be looked into by research as there is a need to rethink the concept of the word in order to hopefully incorporate ALL people regardless of ability, ethnicity, sexuality, religion, etc. Disability is expected to just be that. We aren't allowed to be anything more than our disability it seems, as already established. It's ironic to me that this is the definition of normal, yet from personal experience disability is viewed as strange, and the only way to 'normalise' disability is to bunch every single person with a condition, the same. It's sad, and quite upsetting that there is still this stigma in the twenty-first century, when everything else is finally being accepted into the general public, disability is still not being recognised as a normal way of life. It's always the uncaring discrimination that hurts the most.

One thing I personally experienced which was demeaning, upsetting and depressing was a time where I was labelled by a shop owner. I was young so my wheelchair was small to match my small build just to make a note as it's important. I do wish this was just a story, but sadly it is true. We were out for the day, just mum, dad and myself, when all of a sudden it started raining. There was a shop that

Conclusion

sold collectable dolls houses and furniture etc. This was going to be a hobby of mine as mum and dad bought me a collectable dolls house for Christmas one year, but after my experience, I didn't feel like I wanted to continue with this hobby. I was waiting to go into the shop anyway so we rushed across the road and mum went to open the door as dad went to push me in. There was a step, so dad had to tip my manual chair up for me to get into the shop. All of a sudden, the shop owner came rushing to the shop door saying to mum and dad that they couldn't bring "that in here!" talking about my wheelchair. I was mortified. This was the first time ever in my life that I felt belittled for my condition, this was before the setbacks and backlash that I would face later in life. To be referred to as "that" was an horrible experience to say the least. Regardless of whether they were referring to my wheelchair, what hurt was they never saw me as a person. I was a 'thing'. This was the beginning of my fight to be recognised as an individual; although I wasn't fully aware of the struggles I would have to face just to be seen and treated as a normal human being.

One other horrible experience I have been faced with was being put in the cargo carriage on a steam train with no windows, whilst I took Alisha on a Christmas event with Leanne and her then partner as the train had no disabled facilities whatsoever. Why anyone would think that it would be acceptable to shove a disabled person in the cargo carriage of train with luggage etc., is beyond me. I don't understand. Anything that is created to give people a fun day out, should include everyone. There wasn't any disabled access on the main part of the train which was absolutely disgusting to be honest. Experiences such as these are important for a special needs person's mental health. We should ALWAYS be included in everyday life without feeling a nuisance or inadequate. There should never be any difference between able-bodied people and disabled people.

I have also had some incredible experiences in my life however; seeing and having the wonderful opportunity to meet the Jacksons on a number of different occasions later on in life, years after my twenty-first birthday surprise, all thanks to the Jacksons tour manager being so kind as to make sure I had the best experiences when meeting them. One experience I remember so fondly, as the tour manager made sure the Jacksons came downstairs to meet me when the Meet and Greet

Conclusion

was in a place without a lift, which was sweet of the tour manager to do. Another experience was meeting one of the Jacksons for my birthday in Liverpool (which was a surprise!) Mum and dad arranged it with the tour manager to meet up in Liverpool with Tito Jackson in order for him to sign a photograph that he never had the chance to sign in a previous Meet and Greet. This was a great experience for me as it was so personal. I even had a signed photograph which wishes me 'Happy Birthday' (this is surreal for me, being a fan of the Jacksons for so long, having something so personal to me is extraordinary!) I have now become quite friendly with the Jacksons tour manager. This in itself is incredible! I am extremely grateful for everything the tour manager has done. Thank you, I really appreciate it. I also want to thank mum for this amazing opportunity as she was the one who started it all, by originally contacting the tour manager to arrange for me to attend one Meet and Greet. I would not have had any opportunity or experiences such as this without her arranging it.

Other experiences I have had was going to see Cirque du Solei at the O2 Arena for the 'Michael Jackson Immortal World Tour' and also actually having the incredible opportunity of being where

Conclusion

Michael Jackson stood when he originally made his comeback tour announcement in 2009. This was absolutely amazing for me as only a few years before this, I was sat at home watching the announcement on TV and now I was actually being shown by the O2 Arena staff members where Michael Jackson actually was when he made the announcement. This was a surreal experience.

Other incredible experiences were being asked by Ian and Ceri to be bridesmaid for them, I did cry when they asked me before I said I would! Also, becoming Alisha and Ryan's Godmother and other experiences I will hold a special place in my heart forever as it only cements the fact I am normal.

It may seem as if I have been repeating myself constantly throughout the book. I am not in any way sorry and it was intentional. If I don't try my best to change your mind on how you see disability and mental health, what was the point of writing the book? Basically I've been intentionally repeating myself to drive the point home that we're normal. I'm not saying this book will change the world, I just want something to be out there that tells the full truth about disability and mental health. Not everything out there is the full truth. I

Conclusion

just really want you to understand this and come up with your own conclusions on how to improve things for the better. So, I hope I've done enough to either end any misconceptions or just to get a conversation going on how to better treat special needs people.

Disability is not the be all and end all. We are allowed to be more.

I'm going to speak to every special needs person for a moment as I think it's needed to build back some self esteem that may have been lost along the way. Never let anyone make you feel ashamed of who you are. Be defiant. You are you. You are able, amazing and unique. Own it. Yes, there are some uneducated people out there ready to belittle your abilities, but they will never know the incredible person you are unless you show them. I know it's terrifying, but if you don't take the time to share who you really are and want to be, then it will continue. Be brave enough to say I'm here, this is who I am, this is what I want and by hook or by crook, I'm going to achieve it, because I deserve it! The people who don't believe in you will be the ones who will look silly as you will be breaking the idea of what a disabled person is. Be brave enough to question the treatment of yourself by society. If you don't like how you are treated, speak up! Taking control is the best, most empowering and courageous thing you can do for yourself, but also for others as it will teach them that you do matter. To teach those who have absolutely no belief in your abilities and value, to say "Hey! I'm normal, like it or not, I'm going to prove you wrong! Do you know why!? I have the capability and confidence to do so, that's why! I'm not going to live by your standards anymore! I'm making my own standards of living as my standards encourage self growth as an independent individual!" You have gone through more battles to be included than most and have come out the other side. Never let anyone make you feel anything less than who you are. Like Michael Jackson sang in 'Man in the Mirror": "Make that change."

It took me years to actually have the courage to sit and write this book. Dad always said that I should write a book, but I doubted my abilities. I never thought I had anything interesting to say. What spurred me on to write was Ceri. She asked me to write a review on a book about Cerebral Palsy for her class, that she could then use to teach with, the positivity it gained from everyone after was truly

Conclusion

mind blowing and because of this, I've finally had the courage and confidence to give writing a go, which has been very cathartic to say the least. It's the encouragement from people that everyone requires in order to take a chance and believe in themselves.

I personally want to thank my family for being so supportive whilst writing this book, all of you mean the absolute world to me and I'm thankful that I was brought up in such a loving environment. It may not have been easy for you when I was eventually diagnosed with my CP, but you never showed any sign of struggle. All of you have given me the best possible chance in life all things considered, and I am truly grateful for making me feel loved, happy and above all, normal. Especially these last few years, I know I'm not easy to live with at the moment but with the support and unconditional love I feel, I know I'm finally on my way to becoming my old self again. From the bottom of my heart, thank you I love you all so very much.

Mum has been brilliant throughout all of the recent struggles and prior as she's got the help I need. She's understood everything I am going through and has never shied away with her constant love and support. She's with me everyday and I know it's not easy most days at the moment as my anxiety levels have recently skyrocketed, so I hope she realises how much her support, love and understanding is helping. She's always looked after me in a physical sense, but she's really helping me on a mental sense also. I am feeling stronger everyday just by her encouraging words and unconditional love. Mum I love you more than words can say, and I'm so grateful and I'm so proud that I'm your daughter. I really don't know what I'd do without you. I couldn't wish for a better mother. I love you.

Dad, thank you for planting the idea in my head to write, even if it did take a while to muster the courage to do so. Even if I don't show it often, I do appreciate everything you do for me. In many ways, I wouldn't have got to where I am now without you, (quite literally!) Taking me everywhere I've needed to be without hesitation, like appointments, and then when I've gotten older, to college, university and work, but also taking me on holiday, I've had some incredible experiences in my life and that is mainly due to you actually driving me to have these experiences of which I will never forget. So thank

Conclusion

you Dad, you've made me feel as if I can do anything. I love you.

Ian, thank you for being my older brother. For always being there when I needed you to make me laugh and just act stupid with. You gave me a purpose. You removed those negative thoughts that is associated with disability and replaced it with normality. I'll never forget those days of feeling free and happy with you. You are still the one person who I look up to, even though I'm in my late twenties now. I hope I gave you something to be proud of, as this is all I wanted to do from when I was small. I love you.

Ceri, thank you for making me realise that my opinion matters and for encouraging me everyday since to continue to write. Your support has given me confidence and overall belief in my skills in writing and helped me to focus on something positive instead of just sitting doing nothing. Our recent days out are what I will remember the most. I'm truly grateful and honoured you are my sister-in-law. Thank you. You don't know how much writing has helped to put my life into perspective. I'm just so grateful that you believed in me when I never, pushing me to carry on. You are amazing and inspiring. I love you.

Rosie and Tommy, what can I say about you two? Thank you for being you. When I'm with the two of you I forget all of the sadness and become happy. You both are very special to me. Both of you are caring, kind, considerate, funny and loving. I'm so proud to be your auntie. I just hope you both feel half of the love I feel for you. I love you both ever so much.

Ceri, Rosie and Tommy have been coming along on days out when they are able to lately, which is helping me mentally as I am able to let go of any tension I may have for a few hours, and allow myself to be in the moment and have fun, wherever we are. Sometimes, it's the small shift in mind set for a few hours that give you a calmer demeanour and also equip you with the tools to cope with upcoming events and challenges you may face. It's a reset for your mind set. I am so grateful for all three of them as they could so easily do things without me, but they acknowledge my mental health and are willing to do whatever they can to improve it a little. I want to deeply thank all three of you for helping me through my struggles. I honestly and truthfully do not know where I would be without them at the moment, they are saving me

Conclusion

each time they involve me in plans. It's small things such as this which makes you more strong willed.

Nan, even though you are no longer here anymore, your unconditional love and support alongside your humour will stay with me forever. Your encouragement for me to succeed in life and never give up on myself is something I will always be extremely grateful for. I hope I have done what you hoped for me and made you proud. I love you and miss you everyday.

Granddad Alf, even though I never had the opportunity to get to know you, watching the old baby video of my first birthday makes it clear how much you loved me. I do regret not having theopportunity to get to know you as the stories I hear paints you in a caring and humorous light. I hope I have made you proud and that both you and nan are finally reunited. I love you and miss you always.

Granddad Irving, I hope that the level of pride you showed at my graduation hasn't faltered in any way. Thank you for being you. Your sense of humour and unconditional love is something that I will always remember. I love you and miss you always.

Nanna, again even though I never had the opportunity to get to know you, watching the old baby video of my first birthday makes it clear how much you loved me. I do regret not having the opportunity to get to know you as the stories I hear paints you in a caring and humorous light. I hope I have made you proud and that both you and granddad Irving are finally reunited. I love you and miss you always.

Bubbles, my little pumpkin, thank you so much for giving me all the love I could ever ask for from a pet. You were always there for me to offload all of my troubles when I couldn't off load them to anyone else. I will always be grateful that you were in our family. Your personality was fantastic, making me laugh on my off days just by the little funny things you did on a daily basis. You did more for me at a time when I really needed it. I will always love you and I will always miss you forever.

Leanne, Mark, Alisha and Ryan have their own lives now, so I do not see them that much, but I will always look back on those happy memories.

I just want to take the opportunity to thank my employers for their initial efforts in giving me a

Conclusion

chance to prove myself not only to those who doubted me in life, but for giving me that ability to prove to myself my own worth. So thanks for letting me realise that I am so much more than what people have given me credit for.

I know that I can do anything that I want, despite my disability, and if people don't like me for me, then that is their problem. If people don't show me the respect I deserve, that's okay, because I respect myself too much now for anyone to shatter that. If it takes a lifetime for people to interact with me, either physically or through a text, it doesn't matter at all, it's their loss. I'm more than what people think that I am. I'm now taking control of my life and that feeling of confidence is empowering. I feel strong enough not to depend on anyone but myself. Look after number one and you won't be disappointed with anything or anyone. I know my worth, and my capabilities.

The promises that weren't followed up by actions by a number of people in the past, who cares? I now realise that I don't need these people to make me happy. I can make myself happy. I know what I like, and what I don't like, and instead of always running after those who don't really care, I'm just going to focus that energy into myself and the people who do care about me, which aren't many admittedly, but I rather have a few genuine people in my life, rather than ones who feel sorry for me. I feel so sorry for those people who feel that they

have to make an effort, when they really don't want to. I'm a, strong, independent, intelligent woman who has a lot to offer anyone who wants to be around me.

I also go out now with my mum and her friends whenever I can for the day, and that really helps to keep me on an even keel, we just go for food, but just having a few hours out away from my standard day of working or just in my room is wonderful! A little kindness goes a long way, and my mum's friends are constantly showing me how much they care by just involving me. Thank you mum, June, Janet and Annette for helping me get through the tough times. I will never forget what you are doing for me.

The continuous love and support I have had, especially over the last few years in particular, regardless of how the outside world may see me, has given me the courage and confidence to finally

Conclusion

say without feeling in anyway shape or form, ashamed.

I'm normal, I'm someone's daughter, sister, sister-in-law, auntie, great-auntie, niece and cousin, and I have friends. I also happen to have a sense of humour, I like to have fun, I have coherent thoughts which goes against what it means to be disabled in general opinion. I am not just my disability, yes, my disability is apart of me, but it doesn't define me. My personality defines me. I have people who care for me and people who I can rely on. People who want to be around me.

I also have become more resilient to the people who caused me pain. Learning to let go of all of those negative interactions that I have faced. I am beginning to feel a lot better because of this. These people are not worth my time or my headspace. I have more important things to think about and do, rather than worry about small minded, uneducated and unkind individuals. I used to worry about what people thought of me, as if I wasn't good enough. My self belief never kicked in fully since secondary school. But I got through that and I'm still here, albeit a little bit scarred from a mental aspect due to the whole experience, as well as subsequent experiences since, but I am here and I am really proud of what I have overall been able to achieve in the years following. College helped me a lot; my mental health issues left me during this period, because I was so happy but when I finished, unbeknownst to me, my mental health slowly began to deteriorate.

Everything happens for a reason.

That bullying, constant discrimination and the setbacks, grief and everything else has lead me to believe that I am entitled and worth more than what others may say. It's given me some perspective. I deserve to be happy, my family loves me, I'm a fantastic worker, I have worked extremely hard to achieve everything, (and continue to do so.) As a result, I am proud to be who I am and I'm becoming more comfortable with whom I am as time goes on. I have more than most in my position, a loving family, supportive friends, a job, a support worker, Judi, who I enjoy going out with, as she treats me normal and let's me be as independent as possible, so thank you so much Judi for letting me be me. I truly appreciate you.

All of these things I wouldn't have imagined a few years before. Everything in my life has just given me

Conclusion

the confidence to be stronger and believe in myself. If I don't believe in myself, who else will? You have to earn respect, but earning respect starts with you having to respect yourself first. If you don't respect yourself; nobody is going to respect you. The next step is to demand respect from others by taking chances in life, and if you don't get the respect, move on, those people aren't worth your time, energy or your headspace.

I do feel some sense of guilt however as not all special needs people have the same opportunities that I have been fortunate to have, but this book is somewhat of a stepping stone to help others who haven't been so fortunate as myself.

I have come to a realisation over the years. I believe that because of the backwards thinking I have been subjected to and all of the setbacks that have happened during my lifetime, it has lead me to finally have the courage to also say this: I am not going to be that person that people take advantage of anymore, if people don't like me, that's their problem. I'm not prepared to conform to society's ideals. I'm just me at the end of the day. More than that:

Conclusion

I have Cerebral Palsy, Cerebral Palsy does not have me.